Contents

Foreword

What children learn is important, but how children learn is even more important if they are to become learners for life in today's society. Governments are becoming more aware of the early years as the foundation for future life chances and achievement. This timely and much needed book will help policy makers and practitioners articulate the importance of early childhood as a valuable stage in its own right as well as a preparation for the future.

Respect for babies and young children informs the whole text, together with the recognition that learning is about feelings and relationships as well as thoughts and actions. Engagement in learning through play, the motivating power of children being active agents in their own learning and the role of creativity in learning how to think are all explored. All these are complex and well researched areas. Nancy Stewart brings her wealth of experience and clear thinking to bear on unravelling some of that complexity, and explaining the overarching theme of self regulation, whilst never over simplifying. This is a scholarly approach, but also a practical one – there are examples of what playing and exploring, active learning and creating and thinking critically might look like, as well as key messages for how adults can support children's development as learners.

This book takes us 'back to basics'. There is nothing more basic to effective early years practice than understanding how children learn and early years practitioners have long been proud of being 'child centred'. This book gets to the heart of what that child centeredness really means and why it really matters.

Helen Moylett
President, Early Education
November 2011

Foreword

What children learn is important, but how children learn is even more important if they are to become learners for life in today's society. Governments are becoming more aware of the early years as the foundation for future life chances and achievement. This timely and much needed book will help policy makers and practitioners articulate the importance of early childhood as a valuable stage in its own right as well as a preparation for the future.

Respect for babies and young children informs the whole text, together with the recognition that learning is about feelings and relationships as well as thoughts and actions. Engagement in learning through play, the motivating power of children being active agents in their own learning and the role of creativity in learning how to think are all explored. All these are complex and well researched areas. Nancy Stewart brings her wealth of experience and clear thinking to bear on unravelling some of that complexity, and explaining the overarching theme of self regulation, whilst never over simplifying. This is a scholarly approach, but also a practical one – there are examples of what playing and exploring, active learning and creating and thinking critically might look like, as well as key messages for how adults can support children's development as learners.

This book takes us 'back to basics'. There is nothing more basic to effective early years practice than understanding how children learn and early years practitioners have long been proud of being 'child centred'. This book gets to the heart of what that child centeredness really means and why it really matters.

Helen Moylett
President, Early Education
November 2011

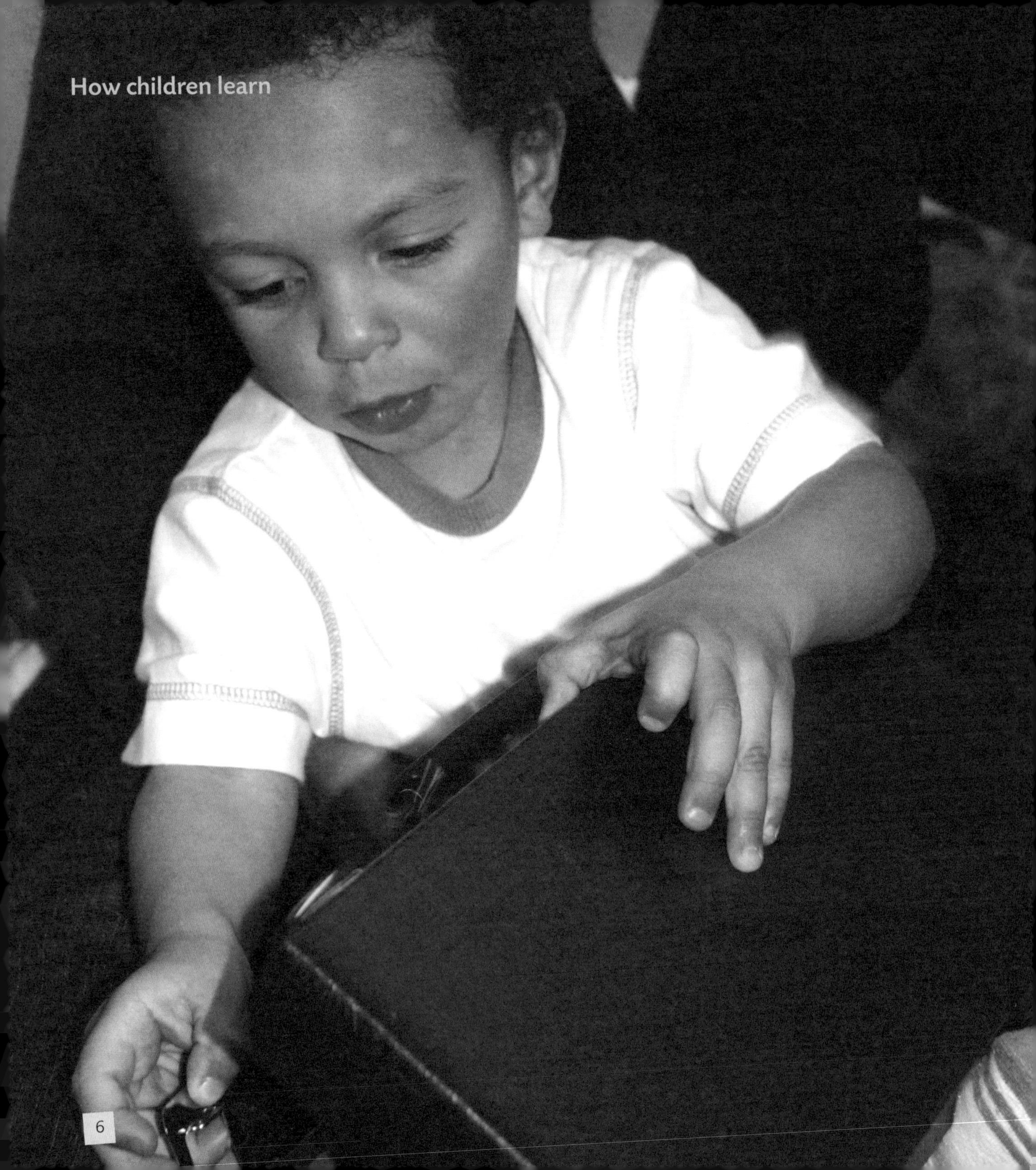

Chapter 1
Introduction

People are remarkable learners. The depth and breadth of our learning is what sets us far apart from all other living creatures, as we develop complex ways of interacting with and thinking about the world around us. At the very beginning of life we learn astonishingly quickly about the physical world, about other people, about who we are and what we can do, and about communicating and using language to shape and share our thoughts.

But beyond what we learn about, in our earliest years we are also building habits of mind that will support us to continue to learn and be successful throughout our lives. Given the right opportunities, we are expanding our powers as learners: We develop belief in ourselves as people who can make things happen. We discover the satisfaction of being interested and involved in activities which puzzle or challenge us. We build confidence to experiment and try things out, knowing that we can learn from what goes wrong as well as what goes right. We don't give up easily when we encounter problems. And we learn not to react just from instinct, but to make decisions about our actions – based on thinking about possible consequences and judging the best way to reach our goals. We learn to picture the future, to predict what might happen, and to control our first impulses if we think waiting will pay off later.

A newborn baby has the roots of all these powerful approaches to learning, and starts to put them into action from day one. Far from the image widely held a century ago of an infant as a 'blank slate' who started out with no abilities,

we now know that infants are putting ideas together and making sense of their world from the very beginning. But how strongly children go on to develop as learners is another matter. A child's development in all areas depends on how inborn genetic patterns interact with their experiences – the stimulation and support that come from other people and the physical world. This is true for becoming an effective learner for life, just as it is for becoming physically strong and healthy.

Childhood is a lengthy period for humans. A wildebeest stands on its own legs within a few minutes of birth and runs with the adult herd in less than two hours, and a newly hatched chick needs only to be shown what to eat and is able to seek food for itself. But a baby is at the beginning of a period of years of being dependent on others. Throughout this long 'apprenticeship' to joining adult society, the young brain is being shaped by experiences that cause frequently-used neural connections to become strong and lasting – giving humans the advantage of great flexibility to develop the abilities and capacities that are proving to be the ones needed in the society in which the child lives. We develop the brains and the minds that our experiences call for.

As adults, we are responsible for ensuring that a child's early experiences are an action call for robust development as a learner. It is important for early years educators to have a clear understanding of what children need to learn – the curricular areas that are needed for success in their society such as language, literacy, ICT, mathematics and so on. But it is not enough for a child to have a particular skill or know some facts. These are of little value in the end without the desire, confidence, motivation and control to use them, and the mental abilities to look at something in a new way, link ideas together and plan and manage the ways forward. To truly support children in their early years to reach their potential, it is fundamentally crucial for the adults who care for and work with children to understand how children learn, and the key role which they play in fostering children's lasting ability to be effective learners and doers across all areas.

Becoming a learner for life

Early years practitioners are committed to providing warm, caring relationships and stimulating opportunities so that young children are happy and engaged in early years settings. At the same time, there is a recognition that children are both being and becoming, and the impact of these early experiences on a child's future is also taken seriously. To enable all young children to reach their full potential is an aspiration commonly stated in early childhood programmes. Early childhood is becoming increasingly recognised by public policy makers as the critical foundation of future development[1], with early experiences having lasting repercussions on social, emotional, physical and cognitive development. Early foundations affect not only how the child succeeds in mastering the immense body of knowledge and skills they will be exposed to throughout their education, but also how successful and fulfilled they will be in their adult lives.

There is a large and growing body of evidence that individual differences in **how** children approach learning are a major source of differences in their achievement in school.[2] Children vary in their dispositions for learning – the habits of mind which include such things as believing in one's own ability to succeed, maintaining a curious outlook, and having a strong motivation to learn. Children also have different patterns of thinking, such as to what extent they set personal goals, make plans, consider how to do things and monitor how well things are going. There is evidence that these differences determine which people will succeed at school and in their careers while others of similar intellectual ability will not.[3] An individual's store of 'grit' – persisting in pursuit of long-term goals – has been found to have no relation to intelligence, and explains why some people are successful while others of equal ability fall by the wayside.[4]

The long-term effects of developing these traits in the early years are profound, and they can be fostered or hindered by their experiences in educational settings.[5] We know that attending early years settings before the age of three boosts children's early attainment[6], and a number of approaches to early education have shown that they can support children's early learning. But supporting children's future development is not just in order for them to make a prompt start with learning in primary school. Looking far beyond to their success as adults is even more important. There is evidence that it is particularly high quality provision which confers lasting benefits for children's achievement as they progress through school[7] and beyond.[8]

So what type of provision will support children as lifelong learners? There are some indications that different approaches to pedagogy bring different results. One study followed disadvantaged children in Chicago and compared the effects of formal direct instruction of skills with a developmentally appropriate approach based on play. The direct instruction group initially showed higher achievement in reading and maths, but as the children progressed into school that advantage disappeared. In the long run, though, there was a strong benefit for the children whose early years experience focused on play: nearly three-quarters graduated from high school, compared to less than half of those with a direct instruction pre-school experience.[9]

One of the strongest sources of evidence of a boost to lifetime success comes from the High/Scope Perry Pre-School project, a rigorous controlled study over a period of 40 years, comparing outcomes for children who participated in the High/Scope programme to those with no pre-school experience and either direct instruction or traditional free play provision. The children were followed from the age of three or four until adulthood. Again, the direct instruction group showed early achievement gains which soon disappeared. By age 15, however, other differences emerged. The direct instruction group were less than half as likely to read books, had engaged in twice as many "delinquent acts," and showed more social and psychological signs of trouble than did those who had attended either a free-play or High/Scope preschool.[10] By age 23, children from the direct instruction group were three times more likely to have been arrested for a felony as those from the other groups, and had eight times the rate of emotional impairments.[11] By the age of 40, the High/Scope children showed significant positive effects across many areas of their lives compared to children who had not attended pre-school. They were more motivated to achieve success in school and willing to work hard in employment. They experienced fewer suspensions from work, fewer arrests and custodial sentences, more stable marriages, less drug use, higher earnings, and higher rates of working as volunteers in their community.[12] These benefits, and their cost savings to society, have often been cited in support of policies of investment in early years.[13]

The question remains, what aspects of High/ Scope and other high quality provision can make such differences to how very young children go on to live their lives many years in the future, not only in relation to their academic learning but also in the many choices they make? There are a number of factors which the High/Scope researchers would point to, including high levels of parent involvement and well-trained teaching staff who support children as active learners who initiate their own activities and construct their own understanding. They also note that several elements of the High/Scope approach link to supporting children to make responsible choices, think for themselves, and plan and organise their activity. Several of these aspects are related to theory and research on self-regulation – how children develop as **self-regulated** learners, and how it affects them in all they encounter and undertake.

Self-regulated learners take charge of their own learning. If we are concerned with making the most of the early years to build foundations for life, it is clear that managing your own learning is a key attribute and possibly becoming more critical than ever. Society, jobs and the skills needed for employment change rapidly, and people need to be ready and able to adapt and learn throughout their lives. There is not one clear predictable path following an education that ends at age 16 or 21, and our future citizens will need to make thoughtful choices, plan ahead, have confidence in their own abilities, and have enough 'grit' to learn in many uncharted ways – online, on the job, by applying existing knowledge in new situations and in different ways.

Self-regulation and emotions

The term 'self-regulation' is used to mean different things, sometimes referring very narrowly only to the ability to manage feelings and control behaviour. Certainly emotional and behavioural self-regulation are crucial elements of success in learning and in life, so a full picture of supporting children as learners must include the emotional aspects. The emotional well-being of young children underpins all development, and must be first and foremost at the heart of what adults provide. The availability of close, warm and consistent relationships with key caregivers who are in tune with and responsive to the child's needs and signals is paramount. Sue Gerhardt in her book *Why Love Matters*[14] provides a thoroughly documented case for putting caring relationships at the heart of care for babies and young children. She describes how the developing brain relies on adults who support the child to regulate emotions, triggering and strengthening the neurological structures which will eventually enable the child to self-regulate and relate to others.

Early attachment and continued warm, authentic relationships are fundamental to development. As we shall see, the emotional climate is integrally tied with further elements of what children need for optimal development as self-regulated learners. Children need to feel emotionally safe to explore new territory, to take risks, to be self-reflective and self-critical, to cope with difficulty and uncertainty – all of which are part of effective learning. They also need to relate well to other people, since social interaction is an integral part of effective learning.

Early years practitioners, supported by early years frameworks, often place an appropriate priority on supporting children's social and emotional development. While there is always room for further developing our awareness and practice in this area, the focus in this book is on additional strands of learning capacity which have more recently come into the spotlight – as seen in the characteristics of effective learning outlined in Dame Clare Tickell's review on the Early Years Foundation Stage.[15]

Self-regulated learning

Developmental psychologists extend the concept of self-regulated learning to cover a number of other areas. There are many different theoretical approaches which define the components somewhat differently, but there are common strands which provide signposts for early years educators to take note of. These are organised in this book into three primary strands, all supported by the underlying basis in social and emotional development:

■ Playing and Exploring – children **engaged** as agents in their learning

■ Active Learning – children **motivated** to learn

■ Creating and Thinking Critically – children **thinking** about their learning

There is much overlap between these strands and each one affects the others. While it is difficult to separate some of the components of self-regulated learning, a many-faceted whole can often be made more accessible by pulling it apart to look more closely at each face. Different theorists have done this in different ways, and identified different links and priorities. The table on the next page describes one simplified way of linking across the complex web of inter-related ideas as they have been described by some influential psychologists and educators. Some of these are described further in later chapters, where they link most closely with the three strands highlighted here. Readers may well be familiar with many of these, and might reflect on the connections that help to establish a clear view of how children learn, and how strongest learning approaches can be fostered.

The strands of self regulated learning

Characteristics of Effective Learning	Relationship and well-being	Playing and exploring Engagement	Active learning Motivation (Will)	Creating and Thinking Critically Thinking (Skill)
Early Years Foundation Stage	Personal, social and emotional development	Play and exploration	Active learning	Creativity and critical thinking
Margaret Carr[16], Te Whariki	Well-being, Belonging	Being ready	Being willing	Being able Working theories
Claxton[17]	Reciprocity	Resourcefulness	Resilience	Reflectiveness
High/Scope	Interaction	Child-initiated learning	Active Learning	Constructivism Plan-do-review
Reggio Emilia	Community	Representation – 100 languages		Creativity Co-constructivism
CHILD[18]	Pro-Social	Emotion, Motivation		Cognition
Accounting Early for Lifelong Learning (AcE)[19]	Social Competence & Self-concept, Emotional well being	Independence	Self-motivation Resilience	Creativity
Psychological theories	Emotional self-regulation, Relatedness	Dewey; Piaget; Vygotsky; Growth mindset (Dweck) Self-efficacy (Bandura)	Mastery goals Self-determination (Deci) Social Cognitive theory	Constructivism (Piaget); Social-constructivism (Vygotsky/Bruner)
A learner's voice	*Is it okay for me to do this?*	*Can I do this?*	*Do I want to do this?*	*How will I do this?*

Agents of their own development

Focussing on how children learn implies a particular way of looking at the relationship between teaching and learning. It turns on its head a view that teaching comes first – that the teacher decides what needs to be learned, tells or presents it to the child, and the child then soaks up the knowledge by remembering what has been said. Few would accept that view of learning for young children, and there is a long and well-established background of developmental theory about young children's learning which places the child at the centre of their learning. Piaget described children's construction of knowledge based on their theories built from experiences of the world and others, and how those theories (or schemas) were gradually enhanced or adapted as children encountered experiences that confirmed or challenged their ideas. Vygotsky and Bruner described the notion of social constructivism, where an adult or more experienced peer supports the child to function just beyond their current level of understanding, scaffolding opportunities for the child to have experiences which call the learning forward.

Children do have an active role – they are not passively receiving knowledge, but are making sense of all the information that surrounds them through their physical experiences in the world, their emotions and sensations, and in relationships with others. Early years practice has made large strides in recent years in identifying the centrality of the learner rather than the content to be learned. In Reggio Emilia, for instance, learning emerges from the children's current ideas and explorations, and teachers plan thoughtfully placed provocations to challenge or expand children's current perspectives. England's Early Years Foundation Stage has successfully supported practitioners in a cycle of first observing children in action, next assessing what this might mean in terms of children's interests and current development, and then responding through planning what the appropriate teaching input would be.

To fully consider children's development as self-regulated learners, however, it is necessary to peel back another layer of the onion to ask: **Why** do children learn? Why are they actively making sense of their experiences? If we understand why children are driven to learn, we can be careful to honour and not to hamper the forces behind their abilities as strong learners.

Key to understanding a child's drive to learn is that it grows from innate, inborn desires. Theorists have described inborn human psychological needs such as:

■ to be competent

■ to make sense of what they experience – an explanatory drive

■ to have autonomy or control

■ to be related to others.

This is the opposite of a behaviourist view which assumes that all learning is shaped by outside influences, with reinforcements or punishments strengthening or discouraging behaviour patterns – training from the outside, rather than making sense from the inside.

Many motivational theorists, however, refer to an inherent need for agency, sometimes referred to as efficacy, mastery, or competence. Agency means the ability to purposefully make things happen. Alongside this, there seems to be a drive to make sense of things by finding consistent and predictable patterns, and to puzzle over inconsistencies – an explanatory drive that pushes a child to test what will happen and especially explore things that don't fit with their current expectations.

Research on the behaviour of infants and children has provided developmental theorists with evidence of inherent drives which appear to be built into our genetic make-up, and are part of the unique learning ability of humans. Martha Bronson, in her comprehensive account of the development of self-regulated learning[20], notes that life itself involves self-regulating systems which manage biological functions and guide development. But rather than just automatically reacting to stimulation and building neural circuits unconsciously, babies are driven to exert conscious control and show delight in mastery of both physical skills and cognitive challenges. Bronson describes experiments with children as young as two months, who developed strategies of turning their heads in certain sequences in order to receive milk. The babies showed displeasure if the outcome didn't match what they expected, and smiled or vocalised when their 'solutions' were correct – and they continued with the activity even when they didn't want any more milk. The researchers concluded that infants have an innate ability to detect patterns in events and feel pleasure from making successful predictions and making things happen.[21]

Very young babies show pleasure in recognising familiar people and patterns in events, and are interested in novelty – they look with renewed concentration at something which is slightly different from what they have come to expect. Recognition of patterns makes it possible to make predictions, and when we can predict we can then plan an action to make something in particular happen. We can begin to cry not from distress because we are hungry, but in order to make our milk arrive courtesy of a familiar caregiver. We can kick our legs and make the mobile swing not by accident, but because we want to see it move – and we will work hard to see that we have been effective.

The innate need to be effective underlies the motivation to learn. Albert Bandura describes a person's belief about whether they can make things happen as **self-efficacy**, and people with a strong sense of self-efficacy show many of the characteristics of effective learners:

- they approach challenges as something to be mastered,

- they develop deep interest and commitment to their activities, and

- they bounce back from setbacks.

People with a weak sense of their own effectiveness, by contrast, avoid challenges believing these are beyond their capabilities, dwell on their limitations, and quickly lose confidence in the face of difficulties.[22] Bandura points out that a sense of self-efficacy grows gradually and can change throughout life. Self-efficacy grows through experiences of 'mastery', and also through social modelling (seeing other people be successful), through relationships which provide encouragement, and through learning how to manage emotional responses to challenge. Unfortunately the reverse processes also apply – self-efficacy is diminished when our efforts don't get results, when we don't have good models, when others demean our efforts. It is easier, Bandura cautions, to dent someone's sense of self-efficacy than it is to build it.

The challenge for early years educators

Over the years when I have advised on interview panels for early years jobs, looking for practitioners who will really make a difference in children's lives, I have noticed a common pattern when I pose the question: Why do you think early years education is important for children? The response is almost always about building social skills – learning to share with other children, being confident to relate to others outside the home – and then secondarily building early skills with number and emergent literacy. Sometimes I ask a related query: Why do you think play is important in young children's learning? The answer there routinely covers what children can learn through their play, with the unlikely suggestion that children playing in the role play house will be diligently counting the cups and saucers or regularly labelling containers in the sand tray as small, medium and large. Of course children do have important opportunities in early years settings to build social skills and confidence, and they do encounter aspects of all areas of the curriculum in their play. But I am still disappointed in these responses because of what is missing.

I am hoping to hear that early years education is important because it can build children's learning power. The right kind of experiences and support can help children to become confident, creative, motivated do-ers and thinkers so that the early years build strong foundations for all they will encounter in the future. I am looking for the practitioner who understands that play is about much more than the content, but also helps to build flexible minds and an enquiring spirit.

Only when we understand the power of the experiences, opportunities and interactions we provide to foster children's effectiveness as learners will we be able to use our knowledge and skills to make this difference. We need to ensure an environment that recognises and celebrates children's growth as learners, and supports them to recognise and value this for themselves. We need to apply our observation and assessment skills to children's development as learners – to consider their strengths, where they need support, and their individual temperaments – and determine the best ways to be enabling partners in children's learning to learn

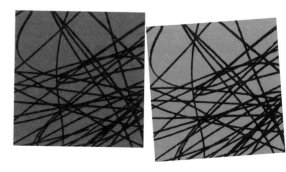

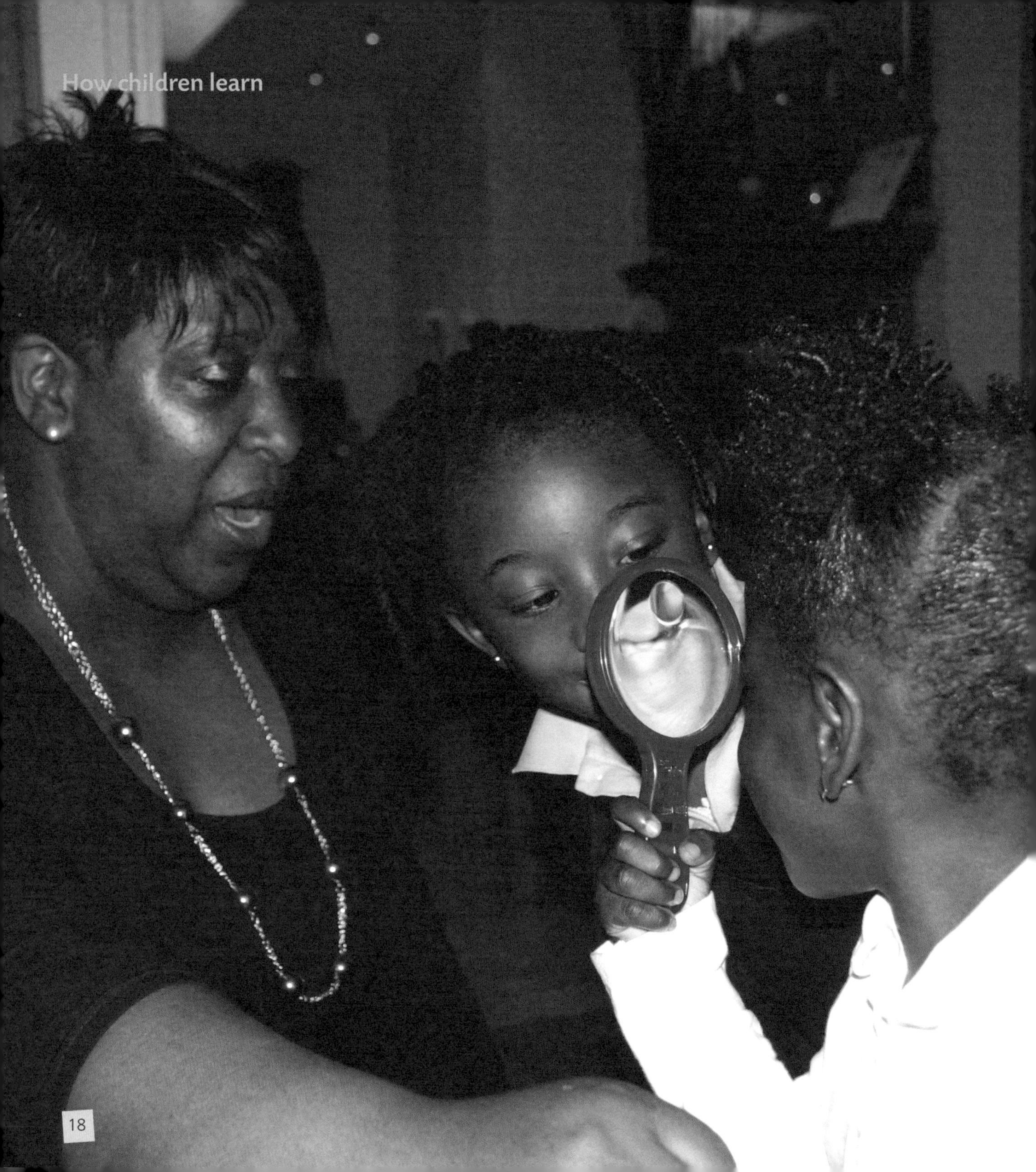

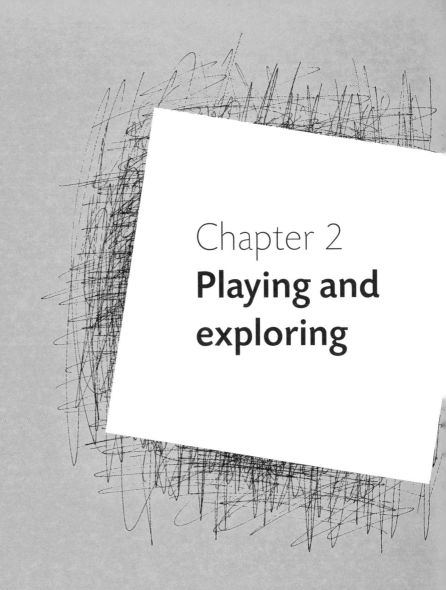

Chapter 2
Playing and exploring

Engaging

Childhood and play go hand in hand, and advocates of play can cite a host of benefits to support children's right to play being enshrined in the United Nations Convention on the Rights of the Child[23]. Play provides healthy exercise and relaxation, and is the stage on which many of young children's social interactions are played out. It also involves open-ended opportunities to explore the world and try things, and if we accept that children learn through their experiences then clearly play is a rich source of raw material for children's learning. Play comes in many forms, from a baby's careful exploration of the items in a treasure basket, to wildly exciting chasing games, to constructing a block enclosure for toy animals or a child-size den from lengths of fabric over tree branches, to pretending to be anyone or anything where anything can happen, to taking turns in games with rules. It can be alone or with others, fleeting or sustained, repetitive or charting new territory.

'Learning through play' is a widely accepted mantra for early years practitioners and policy makers. In a recent major review of the research into learning and development in the early years, the authors conclude that 'Play is a prime context for learning'.[24] Yet exactly how play is related to learning remains an area of wide discussion and differing views. Researchers find that teachers are often uncertain of exactly how children learn through their play and about the role of adults in relation to play – and that the reality of play in classrooms is often far different from the approaches teachers say they use.[25 26]

Policy makers are hearing a message about the role of play in learning to learn. Two UK Members of Parliament who contributed a chapter to a think-tank publication on creativity wrote: 'we know that promoting creativity and play in the early years is actually a first class ticket to producing a creative, prosperous economy many years down the line', and 'play in childhood creates a brain that has greater behavioural flexibility and improved potential for learning later in life'.[27] The 2010 Tickell review of the early years curriculum, however, cites both benefits for learning and a widespread confusion around play: 'It is clear from the evidence that play helps young children to develop the skills they need in order to become good learners – for example helping children to develop flexibility of thought, build their confidence and see problems from different perspectives. However, there is confusion about what learning through play actually means, and what the implications of this are for the role of adults.'[28] The discussion goes on to call for a clearer explanation of learning through 'planned, purposeful play'.

It is no wonder that early years practitioners are uncertain, given the mixed messages they receive. In Wales the Foundation Phase guidance for 3-7-year-olds describes 'play/active learning', and makes a strong case for learning through first-hand experiences. But adult-planned first-hand experiences are not the same thing as play, and the distinction is not always clear. While it talks about free play and the value of exploring and discovering, the Welsh document also says that 'Play should be valued by all practitioners and structured with clear aims for children's learning'[29]. In Northern Ireland, the Foundation Stage calls for children to have 'opportunities to experience much of their learning through well-planned and challenging play'[30].

The question here revolves around how play relates to activity which is 'well-planned', 'structured', and 'purposeful'. If it is planned and structured, is it really play? Does it depend on who is doing the planning and structuring, and who is deciding on the purpose? These are crucial questions, because research which identifies the benefits of play in helping children to become independent and motivated learners may be talking about another thing entirely from adult-planned hands-on activity. What exactly is play, and how does it support children not only to gain specific skills and knowledge but also to be effective learners?

But before we explore further a definition of play, it is important to relieve some of the pressure on the over-loaded word by stating clearly that play is not the only way that children learn. Dedication to 'play-based' learning for young children is not helpful if then the meaning of 'play' is distorted to cover every useful learning experience that children encounter. Certainly children do not identify all of their activity in early years settings as play, even when it is planned by adults as a 'playful' hands-on approach to teaching and learning. Children have been found to be less likely to consider an activity to be play when adults are involved, when the activity takes place at a table, and when they have not chosen it.[31]

Children can learn through all of their experiences, whether play or not. Children learn through imitating what they see others doing, starting from the first day of life when they can already imitate an adult's facial expressions.[32] By one year they can imitate an action they had seen adults doing a week previously without having had any opportunity to try it themselves.[33] They learn through taking part in everyday activities which are not play, particularly when there is conversation about what is going on – for example, riding in a trolley round the supermarket is not play, but can be a rich time for learning with a parent chatting to the child about choices and perhaps giving a task to a toddler such as holding an item carefully or transferring tins onto the checkout. Children learn through stories and talking about pictures in books. They learn through structured activities that adults plan with a particular learning intention. And they also learn through being told about things by people whom they trust.[34] There are many things that children cannot learn through first-hand experience – how their mother is related to their grandmother, for example, or that the sun is much larger than the earth and is a burning sphere. Seeking information from others, fuelled by plentiful 'why' questions, is an important way that children supply themselves with pieces to fit into their growing understanding. Children also learn through directly being shown how to do things, which they can then go on to practise and experiment with for themselves.

Children, then, do not learn only through play. Nor does playing always mean that children are learning. Play can be repetitive, with low levels of cognitive challenge and low levels of real involvement from the child. It can also be frustrating if children lack the skills to do what they have in mind and so abandon their goals.[35] Even the social learning in play is not always positive, as children can be isolated or unable to play cooperatively without support. Skilful and sensitive adults are needed to make the most of the link between play and learning. Effective support for learning through play requires deep understanding of the processes, motivations, and nature of play and playfulness.

What is play?

Play is an elusive concept, which has been defined in many different ways. It could be described in terms of types of activity – such as sensory exploration, construction, physical play, role play – yet the same activity could be play on one occasion but not on another. A child could choose to play with a set of blocks and enthusiastically build a tower one day, and yet not consider himself to be playing the next day when asked to build a tower by an adult.

So play may be less a particular behaviour or activity, and more a state of mind. As Jerome Bruner explained, "The main characteristic of play - child or adult - is not its content, but its mode. Play is an approach to action, not a form of activity".[36]

Play can be described as an activity which:

- is freely chosen and under the control of the player

- is intrinsically motivated – done for its own sake, and not for external rewards

- is open-ended and spontaneous, with the process more important than an outcome

- often involves exploration and imagination

- actively engages the player.

This is what is meant by play which builds children's learning to learn. Perhaps what makes play exciting is the freedom to explore down uncharted pathways, turning this way and that, deciding to continue or change the destination, and alert to unexpected possibilities all along the way. There is no right or wrong to play, so it is safe to try out something new. The child is in charge so play satisfies the need to feel that they are an effective agent in the world. There is also the opportunity to build a sense of personal competence by practising through repeating skills in familiar or new contexts. And play's open-ended scope for choosing what to do and how to do it gives free rein to the need to puzzle over exactly what the child is most interested in making sense of at the moment – so the child is choosing the learning purpose precisely at the edge of their current understanding, and approaching it with keen motivation.

Play has been shown to help to develop these dispositions for learning and habits of mind:

- finding an interest

- being willing to explore, experiment and try things out

- knowing how and where to seek help

- being inventive – creating problems, and finding solutions

- being flexible – testing and refining solutions

- being engaged and involved – concentrating, sustaining interest, persevering with a task, even when it is challenging

- making choices and decisions

- making plans and knowing how to carry them out

- playing and working collaboratively with peers and adults

- managing self, managing others

- developing 'can-do' orientations to learning

- being resilient – finding alternative strategies if things don't always go as planned

- understanding the perspectives and emotions of other people. [37]

Play, starting from early open-ended movement and exploration in response to sensory stimulation and moving into more complex play such as cooperative imaginative play, is an integral part of early development. These experiences build neural connections in the brain and foster flexible, intelligent ways of approaching the world and others. Play researchers describe five types of play categorised around the developmental purposes they serve: physical play, play with objects, symbolic play, pretend and socio-dramatic play, and games with rules. Aspects of these often overlap as children play, and rich play experiences for each child will contain all of these. In the following sections, these five types of play appear in relation to how they support children to be learners.

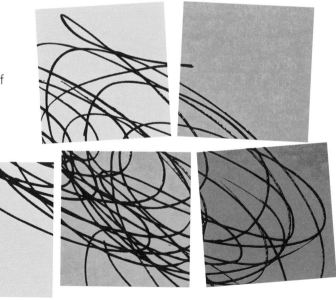

Finding out and Exploring

Joe, 6 months, is on his tummy on the floor, and his mother scatters a range of large shiny seashells of different colours and shapes in front of him. These are new to Joe, and as soon as he catches sight of them he bounces with excitement and reaches toward them. He uses his whole hand to scoop a shell to him, and mouths it briefly. But he is interested in the other shells as well, and waves his arm back and forth through them as they clatter together. His mother says, 'Are they making a noise? You like that, don't you?' For a few minutes he continues to move and mouth the shells, but soon a knobbly shell has got wedged under his chest and he begins to fuss. His mother picks him up onto her lap so he is sitting with three of the shells in front of him, and he continues to move them with his hands as they knock together. He runs his hands over the surfaces, but their broadly rounded shapes are too difficult for him to grip and pick them up. His mother holds one up for him, and he eagerly traps it between his hands and brings it to his mouth.

'All of science is nothing more than the refinement of everyday thinking.'

Albert Einstein[38]

Exploring the world is a powerful preoccupation of young children, who are all born with a keen interest in finding out about objects, events, and people. Babies take in an enormous amount of sensory information, and immediately start to mentally organise their impressions, seeing patterns and making predictions in order to make sense of the world. 'It's not just that we human beings can do this; we need to do it,' say researchers in describing an innate human 'explanatory drive'.[39] The baby who is driven to reach, to taste, to find out about **what an object is** soon grows into the toddler who is driven to manipulate an object to find out **what it can do**, and then into the child who experiments to find out **what can I do with it**?

Relating to the world through their own movements and playing with objects are prime ways that children, like scientists in their experiments, gather data to add to their developing picture of what things are and how the world works. Concepts are built from organising information they gather from their experiences into categories. Before a child can understand the idea of a sphere, and then link it to the name we give a 'ball', she needs experiences of connecting the visual image of a ball with the feel of the round surface, and then with a rolling movement. And to understand what a ball is she needs also to separate it from what a ball is not. She needs experiences of the feel and behaviour of the soft fluffy yellow ball in the baby's crib compared with the soft fluffy yellow teddy bear, and with the big squidgy blue rubber ball. They may feel the same, but what about the shape, and how is that linked to how the object behaves? She can begin to pick out the characteristics that have to do with 'ball-ness' from those that do not.

Like scientists, babies and young children are building theories to explain the things they encounter, and they need to endlessly experiment to build and refine their theories. A scientist can never say that something is definitely true. He can only state his theory, make a prediction of what would happen if the theory is correct, and then test it out. The result of the experiment may be consistent with the prediction – but that doesn't mean the theory is definitely correct. It only indicates that it might be correct, and more experiments will be needed in different situations to build more confidence. On the other hand, if the experiment contradicts the prediction then the theory must be wrong and the scientist will have to go back to the drawing board and adjust the theory to take this new information into account.

Babies only a few months old are able to predict events, such as when and where a ball that rolls behind a screen will reappear out the other side. If the ball behaves as expected, a baby soon loses interest. But she will look much harder and longer when the ball doesn't reappear or rolls out at the wrong time or place.[40] This is puzzling because it contradicts the baby's theory of how a ball behaves in time and space, and something that doesn't seem to make sense captures the baby's intrinsic interest in finding out about and understanding the world. A baby a few months older would be able to crawl or toddle after the ball, and play with it to gather more information about ball behaviour information for herself. The intense busy-ness of a toddler or small child is a

reflection of the need to run a lot of experiments, often repeating things over and over again or in slightly different circumstances, testing how the world works in order to build as reliable a mental map as possible of objects, space, and movement and how these can be affected.

Children are also finding out about other people, so the same processes of recognising a pattern, making predictions and testing them out are important in their interactions with others. A relationship with close, familiar people makes predictions possible, and small babies delight in the playful and predictable to-and-fro of smiley conversations, and in the rhythms they have discovered of anticipation and surprise in peek-a-boo games.

There is also the critical business of building understanding not just of what things are, but also finding out how to actively and purposefully have an effect on objects, events and other people. This relates to innate needs for competence and control (autonomy), and plays a part in children's interactions with the world around them from the very beginning.

Researchers have shown that even in the first weeks of life infants attempt to control their environment. Using sensitive dummies wired to computers, they program a visual display that will respond to the babies' speed of sucking. Babies systematically suck at the rate that will give them a picture of a face which they like to see, compared to less attractive images or no image at all. They also show by their changing sucking rates that they remember later which stimuli they could control and which they could not.[41]

Other studies have shown that very young babies learn that they can make a mobile turn when it is tied to their foot with a ribbon. A week after this discovery they will immediately start kicking with the correct foot when they see the mobile and smile and coo, but do not try the same movements with a different mobile.[42] They have learned where they can make something happen, and are drawn to keep doing the action that makes a difference. When babies have learned that their activity can make something happen, they become angry and unhappy if the mechanism is turned off and their efforts are in vain.[43]

Children's drive to understand and to have control over their environment leads to exploratory play, which is a rich source of learning. Not all children show the same levels of exploratory play, however, and these differences emerge very early in life. One study of 11-12-month old babies looked at individual differences in their exploratory behaviour, and linked it to problem-solving abilities. The researchers found differences not only in the depth in which children explored, but also in the breadth – the range of ways of exploring and the things explored. They found that those who explored more overall were those who explored in most breadth, and these babies also showed more successful and complex problem-solving.[44] So 'having a go' in playing and exploring, which will be considered later in this chapter, is linked with developing problem-solving abilities from a very early age.

It is not surprising that children who explore more readily and widely in their play develop greater problem-solving ability. They have many more opportunities to try out multiple ways of doing something and to learn from trial and error,

finding out in the process that it is worth sticking with a puzzle because there may be a solution in the next thing they try. Jerome Bruner believed that developing flexibility of thought was at the centre of play. In experiments where children were given practical problems to solve, those who were given a chance to play with objects first were more inventive and stuck with the problem, often finding a solution in repeated efforts if they were unsuccessful at first. In contrast, those who were simply taught how to use the objects either remembered what to do and solved the problem immediately, or gave up the effort.[45]

Why do some children engage in more exploratory play than others? Inborn temperament is a factor, with some children genetically inclined to show high activity levels and to try new things. Others, by contrast, are by nature more placid and tend to withdraw from unfamiliar experiences – these children prefer to look before they leap, and would rather watch someone else have a go and weigh things up before having a hands-on experience. Elements of temperament are traits which are fairly stable throughout life, and sensitive adults understand the child's temperament and respond and support in ways which are appropriate for the individual child. Developing as a player, as with all areas of development, is shaped by the interaction of inborn tendencies with the experiences a child encounters, and adults have an influence which can either encourage or discourage children from playing to find out for themselves. Sensitive encouragement and modelling of exploratory behaviour can support hesitant children to experiment more, while exuberant and distractible children can be encouraged to focus attention and explore more carefully.

Adult role in exploratory play

There is a finely balanced relationship between adult involvement which supports a child to explore, and which becomes intrusive and discourages the child's own explorations. This is the key dilemma facing early years practitioners when they consider their role in supporting children to learn through play: Can they enter the child's activity in a way that will help the child to notice, to discover, to wonder, to experiment more? Or will adults inadvertently squash the spontaneous nature of play and lessen the child's sense of freedom and control, removing its power to motivate and intrigue young learners?

Parents have an effect on children's play behaviour for many children long before they are involved in early years settings, while for babies in daycare provision the caregiver also influences dispositions to play. A long-range study looked at children from the age of nine months to twelve years, and linked children's levels of exploration and competence with parental support. Parents who were more responsive had babies who explored more, showing more competency at age nine months. For boys particularly, parents who were responsive while respecting the child's autonomy supported the early development of competence, and early individual differences remained stable from babyhood through childhood.[46] It is a matter of being tuned in to child's signals to see what the child is interested in and trying to do, which helps the adult see how to support the child in their own explorations. This is very different both from not noticing and offering no support, and from being controlling and showing the child what to do.

Parents and trusted caregivers offer children a safe base from which to explore, knowing that help is there when needed, but it is important to expect that children will do some exploring on their own. The 'helicopter parent' who hovers over the child's every move and interacts at every opportunity is doing the child no favours in their development as independent learners. Mothers who are responsive but do not instantly answer children's requests have children who independently explore more, and so become more competent. By contrast, babies and toddlers whose mothers constantly initiate activities and control how they are done – such as showing the 'right' way to use a toy – become less likely to initiate explorations themselves, and show less competence.[47]

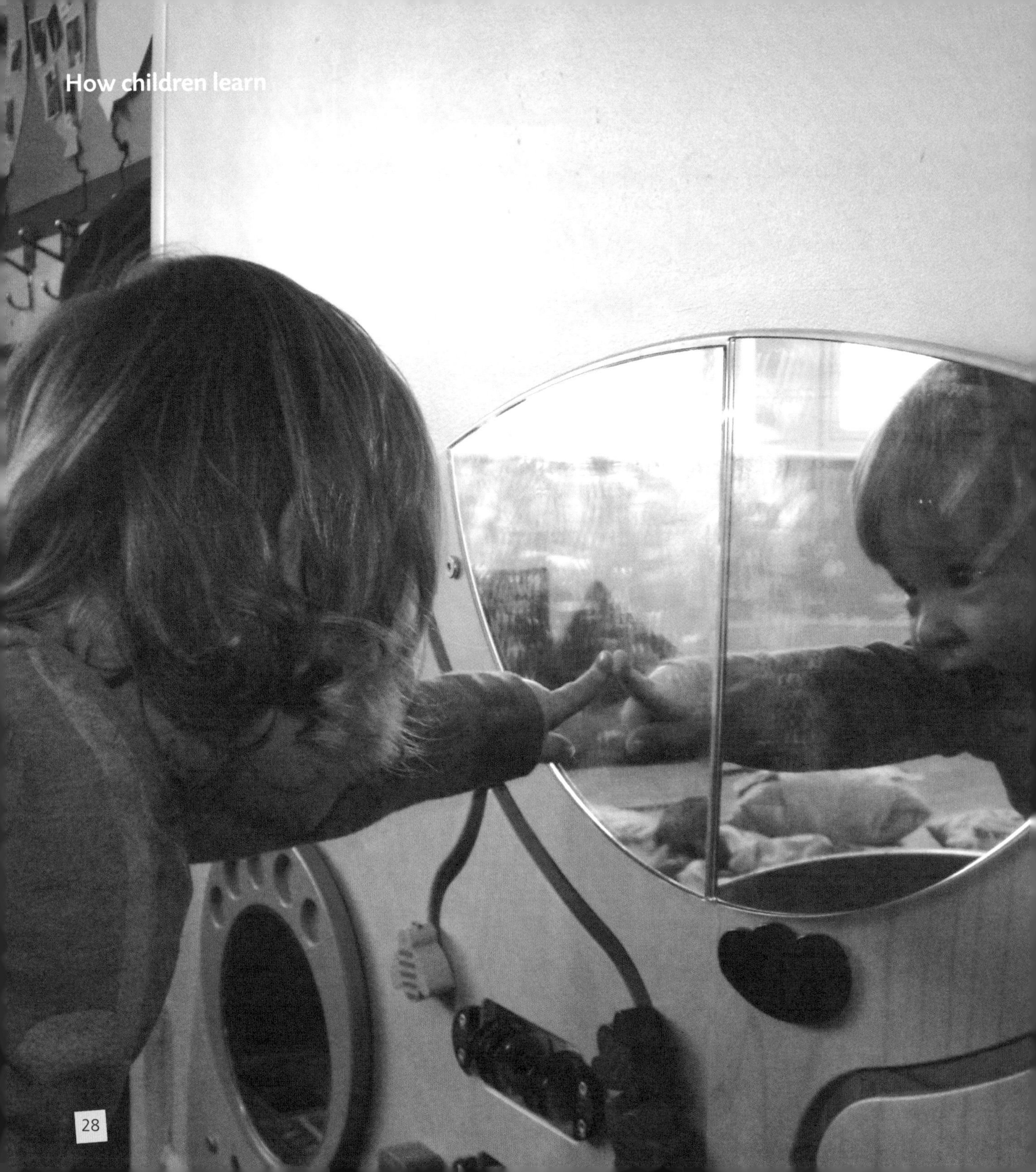

The same limiting effect of showing children how to do things was highlighted in recent research looking at the relationship between direct instruction and modelling spontaneous exploration and discovery. In one experiment, four-year-olds were shown a toy with four tubes which each did something interesting – such as squeak when pulled, or show a hidden mirror inside. With some of the children, the researcher showed the toy and pretended to be surprised when she found that pulling a tube made it squeak. With other children the researcher was more direct, deliberately showing them how to make the toy squeak. When left alone to play with the toy, the children who were 'taught' how to make the toy squeak focussed on copying that one action. But the children who saw an example of discovery learning played with the toy longer and discovered for themselves more of its other hidden features.[48]

Another recent study found that more original thinking resulted from observing playful exploration rather than being directly shown how to do something. The researcher showed 4-year-olds a toy, and performed sequences of three actions – some sequences made the toy play music, and some did not. She showed nine sequences, five which worked and four which did not, with the toy playing music only when the last two actions in the sequence were the same. The children were then given the toy and told to 'make it go'. The only difference between what two groups of children saw was that with some children the researcher pretended not to know how the toy worked, while with others she acted as a 'teacher', showing them how it worked. Many of the

children who had seen an exploration of the toy discovered the most efficient way to make the noise – using only the two key actions instead of three, which they had not been shown – while those who were taught how it worked imitated all three actions and didn't find the more intelligent solution.[49]

While children's exploratory play is triggered by their own interest and can be hampered by too much adult input, there is still an important role for adults in fostering exploratory play. While the direction a child's exploration takes is spontaneous and cannot be pre-planned, adults have a key role in planning for play. Providing a rich environment full of interesting things will help to stimulate investigation. Children are impelled to find out about things which are not too familiar and not too strange – but are just enough different from what they would expect. For a small baby, this might mean creating within the child's reach a mobile with just two or three objects, and then varying the number or another characteristic. For example, add another spoon to a set of two already there, or change a metal spoon for a wooden spoon. Toddlers want to explore how things work, so objects that can be manipulated in different ways are intriguing and satisfying. Soon children will want to explore how things can be combined or arranged in various ways, so open-ended materials that can be stacked, put inside each other, and moved by cause and effect are likely to be interesting. As open-ended exploratory play moves on to finding out how to reach certain goals, such as building with construction items, a wide range of materials that can be fastened together and combined in many ways enables free experimentation.

Development is sometimes thought to move from earlier to later stages, but just because we have moved onto finding out how things work and how we can make them behave does not mean that we have left the earliest stages behind. We don't so much leave early stages, as layer on increasing ways of engaging with the world, building our repertoire of ways to learn. Sensory exploration of unfamiliar materials and objects remains important, so an environment that encourages hands-on experience of unfamiliar things encourages learning.

Adults planning an environment that encourages exploration will need to be aware of the dangers of sensory overload. Being bombarded by sensory information from all sides discourages exploration, as does a chaotic environment. Open space, uncluttered room to focus on one thing at a time, and a calm atmosphere without too much noise all contribute to rich exploratory play. Regular tidy-up time, in homes as well as early years settings, helps to provide a fresh canvas for the child to decorate with their next explorations.

Uninterrupted time to explore is another necessary ingredient, along with freedom to move and combine materials to find out what they can do in unexpected situations. Like scientists, children at play need to experiment in new directions in order to make significant discoveries.

Having helped to set the scene for children to follow their own fascinations, it is important that adults do not then totally withdraw and leave the children to it. Discovery is enhanced by sensitive, just-enough interactions. Adults can sometimes spark an initial interest, perhaps

demonstrating one element briefly and then withdrawing in favour of the child's independent exploration as soon as the child is engaged. They might even show a particular way an object might be used, as long as it is offered in the spirit of possibility and not direction – such demonstrations can offer a way in for children to begin to interact with unknown things, described by one writer as offering 'a flashlight in a cave' as 'the child uses the flashlight to discover new and interesting things, which sparks further curiosity'.[50]

Adults may also support children's explorations by offering a small prop as needed to enable the child to manage what they are trying to do – watching closely to understand the child's intention, and judging whether or not to support when the child is having difficulty. As we shall see in looking more closely at developing persistence, children need experience of dealing with difficulty in order to become resilient learners who do not give up easily. Skilful, tuned-in adults decide whether the child can manage the level of challenge in what they are attempting to do and will rebound to refocus their exploration as needed, or whether they are likely to become frustrated and give up without a judicious and non-intrusive helping hand.

Finding out and exploring, then, provides a first-hand basis for children to gather information about the world and other people, and to build and refine their theories about what everything is, what it does, and what they can make it do. It provides the raw material for children to combine in new and original ways as they develop more complex ways of playing.

Playing with what they know

Amber, age 4, has planned to play 'dressing up' with two friends. She pulls a skirt over her clothes and wraps a shiny cloth around her shoulders, while her friends choose what they will wear to transform themselves into someone else. Her friends say, 'We're going to the ball, and you have to stay here.' Amber busies herself with setting out containers on a counter. A visitor to the setting, Jennifer, approaches and Amber says, 'I have to do all the work. I have to do the cleaning and cook every day.' 'Do you? Why do you have to?' asks Jennifer. 'Because my mother is really mean. Well, it's not my mother really, it's the two ugly sisters who make me do all the work.' She continues lining up containers, and then adds, 'I'm Cinderella.' 'I thought you might be,' says Jennifer. Amber looks at her carefully, then puts her hand over her mouth to say in a whispered aside, 'I'm really Amber, you know.'

'When I examine myself and my methods of thought I come to the conclusion that the gift of fantasy has meant more to me than my talent for absorbing positive knowledge.'

Albert Einstein[51]

A wonderful ability appears in children's play, often early in the second year of life. The internal questions the child is exploring in play move from **'what is?'** to include **'what if?'**. This is the root of all human creative invention, and the marker of intelligence that lifts us out of the here-and-now to be able to imagine other possibilities. It is only when we can imagine something different from present reality that we can plan what we need to do to create something new. Imaginative play, behaving 'as if', is also intimately tied to understanding other people, developing empathy and being able to effectively communicate thoughts. The player is asking: *What if this box could be a bed? What if we didn't have to stay on the ground, but could fly through the air? What if I were my mother – how would I feel, what would I think and understand?*

Increasingly complex play is linked in a reciprocal way to the development of the cerebral cortex, the part of the brain governing cognitive functions. Rapidly wiring neurons make it increasingly possible for the child to control impulses and attention, to remember ideas, to be more aware of consistency or inconsistencies. This growing cognitive ability enables the child to develop play that is not just exploratory in the moment but is aimed toward a goal – to solve a problem or manage a particular task – or which requires re-combining ideas from their past experiences. And the more the child plays in a way that engages these cognitive capacities, the more those synapses are reinforced and the brain becomes increasingly able to support complex activity and self-regulated learning.

Parents often support a child's imaginative thinking as they model the beginnings of fantasy play. 'Is Teddy tired? Shall we tuck him in bed?' they may say to a toddler. When offered a bite of a sticky, well-gummed piece of bread, they may smack their lips together as if nibbling and say, 'Yum-yum-yum. Thank you,' starting a hilarious repetitive game in which it is clear to both players that they are not really eating. What is happening in these exchanges is such second nature that we have often, as Vivian Gussin Paley describes, 'confused the extraordinary with the mundane.'[52] For a child who is beginning to pretend is taking a fundamental cognitive leap. They are making something stand for something else – a stuffed toy for a live and sleepy friend, a 'yum-yum' sound for eating – and this is the beginning of symbolic thought.

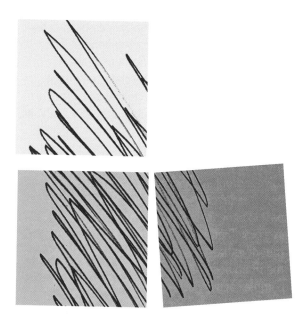

The power of symbols

Symbols help us to hold ideas in our mind, separating them from their material reality, which enables us to imagine things differently and to put them together in different combinations. We don't have to physically pour tea into the cup and feel it in order to know it will be hot, but we can create and hold an image of that experience in our minds. A child who has never handled hot tea, but has poured other liquids and may have tasted other foods that were a bit too hot for comfort, will be able to put those ideas together in make-believe play to pour non-existent tea into a cup, sip from the cup and react to the hot sensation in their mouth. The child is able to behave as if the tea were a steaming liquid in the pot, drawing on the ideas in their mind.

Early pretend play for one- and two-year-olds usually involves pretence with objects which look much like what they are representing – such as a toy pot, spoon and plate for serving a meal. By age 3-4, they will be able to imagine more fully, and could create a meal cooked in a bucket, stirred with a stick, and served onto a large leaf. In both cases, though, the child knows that the object they are using stands for something else – for an idea that they are representing in their pretend play.

Vygotsky believed that the ability to use symbols was the cornerstone of the human ability to think. Various 'tools of thought' which allow us to represent our thinking enable us to develop complex abstract ideas, to share them with others, and develop culture. Prime among these representational tools is **language**. Other ways of representing thoughts include such things as mark-making, drawing and painting, music, movement, sculpture, dance, drama. The refinement of thinking through representing ideas and experiences in a variety of ways, using each transformation of the idea into a form of expression as an opportunity to clarify the thinking, lies at the heart of the Reggio Emilia concept of the 100 languages of children. For Vygotsky, representing ideas in pretend play was a critical bridge from the concrete world of the young child's sensory exploration to the possible worlds of abstract thought.

Intriguing evidence of increased flexibility of thought in the world of make-believe comes from studies of young children's ability to make logical deductions. Children respond very differently when they are in fantasy mode or not, when faced with logical puzzles such as:

All cats bark;
Tot is a cat;
Does Tot bark?

Five-year-old children generally say no. A cat that barks is outside of their life experience, and they rely on what they have found out through exploration of **what is**. But when the researchers first encourage them to pretend ('Let's pretend that all cats bark...') then the children are able to follow through to the logical conclusion that Tot barks.[53] In the world of **as if** children are able to accept the initial information, and then can use abstract thinking about consequences to make the connection to the correct answer.

Practice in this type of thought is essential if children are to develop as thinkers who don't jump to conclusions which might appear obvious, but instead are prepared to suspend judgement and think things through, considering other ways of looking at a problem and being aware of the different consequences that arise from different starting points. Aristotle has been quoted as saying, 'It is the mark of an educated mind to be able to entertain an idea without accepting it.' This ability to play with ideas, to weigh them up and consider from all angles, is supported through pretend play.

The rules of play – developing self-control

While to a casual observer it may seem that children involved in pretend play are acting totally spontaneously in 'free play', in fact they are imposing their own set of rules. A child playing with a small world farm will drive the tractor around the fields and carefully into the barn, but he is unlikely to make it fly. I once observed three children in a home corner, sitting on a sofa and staring intently at an empty box which was their television. One had possession of the 'remote', represented by a wooden block from a construction set, and they periodically engaged in heated discussion about whether to change the channel because they wanted to watch different programmes, or whether the volume should be turned up or down.

Through experiences like these children practice their growing self-control and learn to govern their impulses – to think before they act. Giving a particular meaning to an object or situation, and especially personally taking on a role, involves accepting boundaries on how to behave. Mothers and fathers go to work and make the dinner, but not babies. Babies cry, while grown-ups take responsibility for caring for and calming the babies. Even fantasy characters behave according to some rules. They may or may not be able to fly, and their magic weapons have some powers but not others. The limits may change as the play progresses, and children may continually re-define who they are and what is happening, but then it is necessary to acknowledge an author's re-write: 'No, you be the monster. Pretend I'm flying and I have

my zapper.' Children who show self-restraint in following the shifting rules of the play gain the great pleasure of belonging, as they develop cooperative play with others.

Orderly games with rules can also be introduced to children at a very young age. In some ways, they are an extension of early turn-taking exchanges and games like peek-a-boo that have an orderly structure. Board games with players taking turns, perhaps with a spinner or dice followed by moving a piece, or lotto games where covering a square follows a rule and a particular sequence, help children to learn to control their impulses and regulate their behaviour within a structure that they can understand.

One particularly strong support for children in developing cognitive self-control is the use of language. As children begin to mentally tell themselves what to do, rather than just reacting impulsively, they use words to make their thinking clear to themselves. Private speech – children talking aloud to themselves as they describe what they are doing and tell themselves what to do next – has been linked with internalising messages from others about strategies, values, and skills and gradually making these their own. Young children use this self-talk to work through their ideas, to consider obstacles, to remind themselves of skills, and to manage their emotions. Private speech is a feature in most activities for young children but is particularly prominent in imaginative play, possibly because pretend play provides an endless stream of challenges to thinking and behaviour as children encounter or create problems to be solved.

In early simple dramatic play, children begin to represent concrete actions they have done themselves such as eating their dinner, or seen others do such as driving a car. Moving into more complex socio-dramatic play, however, brings additional cognitive challenges that further develop thinking abilities. A plot is developed, with a sequence of events and a range of problems to be solved. The players need to meet the challenges of negotiating different roles, considering different perspectives both of the characters and of the real life players, and remaining open to the 'as if' thinking of others. Pat Broadhead, researching social and cooperative play, has demonstrated the high cognitive challenge for children involved in cooperative role play particularly when it is open-ended – using a range of versatile resources in what she has called the 'whatever you want it to be place'.[54]

Make-believe play has been shown to contribute to self-regulation, with greatest benefits for the most impulsive children. Working with three- and four-year-olds from middle-income families, researchers looked at changes over several months in elements of self-regulation including independently tidying-up and attention and cooperation during circle time. When they controlled for other factors such as language ability, they found greater improvement in self-regulation among the children who had spent more time in complex socio-dramatic play – including pretend representation of objects, cooperating with others, and talking in role as characters.[55]

When the same researchers, however, looked at deprived children in Head Start classes in the United States, they did not find a benefit of make-believe play for children's self-regulation. They noted that among these children much of the play content was violent, and cited other research linking aggressive behaviour and violent play themes. They also note other research indicating that children with violent fantasy themes may have more models of aggressive behaviour in the home, while the children who used non-violent play themes developed more complex cooperative narratives in their play.[56] There has been much consideration in recent years about play themes, most often employed by boys, which involve superheroes, weapons and often boisterous activity. Penny Holland, in her book *We Don't Play with Guns Here*[57], has challenged practitioners to reflect on their practices in respecting children's play themes, while acknowledging the role of the practitioner in supporting this play to move beyond repetitious physical activity.

35

Children who consistently use the toy dinosaurs simply to make loud roaring noises and bash them together, for example, will not be making significant headway in learning to think through and control their actions. An adult may, however, be able to join the play and enrich the narrative through introducing another dimension to the play – the dinosaur might cry, or need some help because he's hurt, or perhaps he's really hungry and wonders how he can get enough leaves to fill his big stomach, or he could be looking for his friend.

This is a useful reminder that it is not enough to assume that when children are playing, they are learning – and nor are they necessarily developing their learning potential. Play skills develop over time and often children who are older or more skilled players support others to join in, scaffolding development of more complex play. Where this is not occurring, however, early years practitioners can sensitively enhance the complexity of the play to enable children to benefit. A skilled adult can judiciously join in with fantasy play and act as a play tutor, modelling and sparking ideas about problems to solve, extending ideas about characters, settings and props, and supporting cooperative negotiation about how to play.

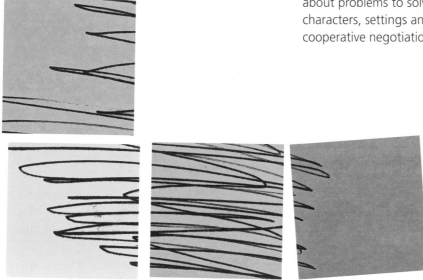

Being willing to 'have a go'

Rahim, age 3, wants to join in the task of moving some shrubs to another area of the nursery garden. He finds a small trowel and pushes it into the hard, dry soil, managing to dig a small hole. Then he picks up an adult spade. 'I can use this,' he says, though it is difficult for him to balance upright and he makes little impression on the soil. Kelly, the practitioner, asks if he would like her to show him how he can push it harder. He agrees, and she demonstrates using a foot to push down on the spade. Rahim confidently takes the spade back, and tries first standing with one foot on the spade, and then begins to jump onto it. He is rewarded with sinking a few inches into the soil, and lifts the soil out successfully. On his next attempt he overbalances and tips over with the spade onto the ground. 'Never mind,' he says as he dusts off his knees and goes back to work.

'Life is like riding a bicycle. To keep your balance you must keep moving.'

Albert Einstein[58]

If the main arena for children's learning is their interactions with people, objects and events in the world, then a strong disposition for learning must include the urge to seek out experiences. A child who readily takes part in opportunities that present themselves and also initiates experiences for himself will have a larger store of information to learn from than a child who holds back, wary of trying something new and unwilling to take a risk. Although all children have an innate drive to participate with others and in the world, children differ in the degree of willingness to have a go. Differences arise partly as an aspect of inborn temperament but are also influenced through messages transmitted by their caregivers from their earliest days.

Innate drives for making sense of the world – an explanatory drive – and for competence and autonomy all have a part to play in children's willingness to have a go. Curiosity is seen in people who want to explore and feel a need to satisfy their mind about something new, which I will consider in a later section on motivation for Active Learning. For children to become engaged in activity which can satisfy their curiosity, however, they need to feel competent and able to participate. While some children have a strong 'can do' attitude that launches them into challenging situations where they are seeking mastery, others lack the confidence to try and are victims of what researchers have called 'learned helplessness'.

A 'can do' attitude, even when unrealistically optimistic about what can be accomplished, may be an important basis of accomplishing something new. Arthur Bandura has developed a theory of self-efficacy beliefs, the personal beliefs about whether one is capable of reaching their goals in particular situations. He writes that most unrealistic beliefs people hold are over-estimates of their capabilities, and that this is a benefit: 'If efficacy beliefs always reflected only what people can do routinely they would rarely fail but they would not set aspirations beyond their immediate reach nor mount the extra effort needed to surpass their ordinary performances'.[59] In other words, our reach should exceed our grasp. In contrast, Bandura describes the anxiety and depression that arise for those who do not feel they can manage difficult situations.

It is not unusual to see a small child diving into an activity with full expectation of success – a hefty whack of the egg on the side of the bowl leaving fragments of shell and egg white oozing between fingers, a too-large milk jug at the snack table wobbling uncontrollably when hefted by small arms, shoes with toes pointing outward confidently fastened on the wrong feet. Adults may offer judicious support to enable children to be successful in managing challenging tasks, but it is crucial to honour the belief in personal competence that the child brings. Experiences of mastery help to maintain and build belief in competence, so the child should be aware that they were in charge and accomplished the task, with the adult offering minimal support and withdrawing as soon as possible.

Having a positive attitude to opportunities and challenges creates a virtuous circle. The more we think we can, the more willing we are to try something new. We then learn through the experience and become more competent still, and more ready to enter into new challenges. We might even have an effect on what might be seen as luck – where chance intervenes with our degree of personal control in our lives. Bandura explains that people 'can make chance happen by pursuing an active life that increases the level and type of fortuitous encounters they will experience. Chance favours the inquisitive and venturesome who go places, do things, and explore new activities.'[60]

Supporting children to believe they can

Children are highly attuned to the messages important caregivers give them about opportunities or threats in their environment. This is a crucial evolutionary trait that helps to keep dependent children safe as they learn to negotiate their environment. When confronted with something new, babies from nine months of age use a strategy known as **social referencing** to check with their caregiver whether or not it is a good idea for them to engage. They search the face of someone they trust and listen carefully to the tone of voice, looking and listening for signs of encouragement or concern.

One example of experiments with social referencing involved confronting crawling babies with a visual cliff – a plexiglass surface which was safe to crawl over, but which looked as though there was an edge falling sharply down into a gap between the baby on one side and the mother and appealing toy on the other side. The babies stopped at the visual edge, and looked at their mothers for a clue about this unknown situation. When the mothers made a fear face, the babies stayed securely on the edge and did not cross the divide. But when the mothers smiled encouragingly the babies typically crawled across the space.[61]

Through social referencing babies and young children are reading the emotional cues of a trusted adult to tell them whether or not to explore, and they remember these lessons. One study found that even when mothers did not give a sign on a subsequent occasion, the babies still avoided the toys that they associated with a negative message. They did not generalise this, however, and played readily with other toys.[62]

The message for adults is that supporting children to explore through giving encouragement with voice and body language can broaden the range of a child's explorations and experiences, while showing negative feelings such as worry, fear or disgust will establish avoidance patterns in the child for those experiences. That is right and appropriate if we are helping children learn to recognise and avoid real dangers. But how often do adults pass on negative messages which are unnecessary and which limit the child's sense of themselves as competent explorers? How many children who would have been fascinated by watching a spider move up and down its strand of web or scuttle across the floor have been put off by an adult's discomfort with spiders? How many children have been stopped by adult concerns from testing and challenging the limits of their balance when walking along a low ledge?

Keeping children safe is of course a central responsibility for adults who work with children. But children learning how to assess and manage risks is an essential part of eventually managing their own safety, and they need experiences at the limits of what they can do in order to know their own capabilities. Active physical play including rough-and-tumble, particularly in challenging outdoor spaces, helps children to test their limits and understand their capabilities, as well as to relate to the needs and perspectives of others. Adults often feel uncomfortable with rowdy play, fearing that it may tip over into fighting, but children are not being aggressive in rough-and-tumble play and are actually learning about exercising control.

Cutting off children's explorations with over-protective concern sets their boundaries too narrowly so that they miss learning opportunities, and it also may establish a negative attitude to risk which can have further-reaching consequences for the child as a learner. An effective learner is ready to take risks, accepting that the unknown always involves some risk and that things which don't go as expected can teach us as much as those that do. The message we need to give children is that a failure is not something to be avoided, but is both evidence of engagement and an opportunity to learn.

Learned helplessness versus mastery orientation

Unfortunately the attitude some children have developed from their experiences is not 'can do', but 'I can't'. Researchers call this learned helplessness, first identified in animals who were put in unpleasant situations over which they had no control and then later made no attempts to help themselves even when they could have escaped. Learned helplessness in people can begin very early in life if children cannot see any effect of their actions on their environment. An important aspect of the child's experiences – both with the physical world and with other people – is contingency, which is the child perceiving that things happen in direct relation to the child's actions. In extreme cases learned helplessness results from neglect or caregivers who do not respond in a contingent way to a child's signals and activity. In effect, a child stops trying because experience has taught them that their actions will not be effective.

The effect of learned helplessness was shown in an experiment with young babies where one group was placed in cots with sensory pillows connected to mobiles which the babies could control by turning their heads. The other group could not affect the movement of the mobile, but only look at it. When both groups were then put in cots that allowed babies to control the mobiles, only those whose movements had previously had an effect tried to use the pillow – the others had learned that there was no point.[63]

Toddlers are eager to make an impact on their world, and need experiences where their autonomy is clear to them. By age two some children already show signs of helplessness, giving up easily and being reluctant to engage in new activities. Sensitive adults who support a child's autonomy have an important role in contributing to the child's perception that they are effective. Studies have found that children as young as 12 months show more mastery behaviour when their mothers show sensitivity and support for their child's autonomy in accomplishing what they wanted to do, while more controlling mothers who stopped the children's actions and controlled how they used things had children with less motivation toward mastery with toys.[64]

Carol Dweck has investigated the underlying thinking of people who show a mastery orientation compared to those with learned helplessness, and has identified the positive role of what she has called a 'growth mindset'. In studies with 10-year-olds, Dweck and colleagues gave the children problems to work on and afterwards praised some of the children for their intelligence, and others for their effort. When offered the choice of more challenging tasks, those praised for effort chose the challenge while those praised for their intelligence opted for an easy option. Dweck hypothesises that those praised for their intelligence were fixed on the successful outcome in order to maintain their image as intelligent and so avoided a risk of failure, while those praised for effort valued the chance to learn. When the researchers then gave the children much harder tasks, those praised for their intelligence thought that experiencing difficulty meant they were not intelligent, and said they no longer enjoyed the task and didn't want to practise at home. Those praised for effort, however, realised that a harder task required harder work, enjoyed the task and chose to practise.[65]

The link with learned helplessness lies in where people see the locus of control – either in themselves as something they can have an effect on, or as outside their control. When people have a **growth mindset** they see their ability as something over which they have control – they can try harder, and through doing more they will develop greater abilities. People who show learned helplessness, on the other hand, have a **fixed mindset** and think they have the level of ability or intelligence they were born with and cannot change it. They think there is nothing they can do about their performance, and whether they do well or not has nothing to do with them – it's a matter of luck, fate, or the control of others who have power over the situation. In fact, while intelligence and talent do have some genetic basis, variability from experience and practice far outweighs inborn patterns in determining how far potential develops. As the American inventor Thomas Edison said, 'Genius is one percent inspiration and ninety-nine percent perspiration.'

Being a learner is not always easy, which is an important message for learners to hear. People with a fixed mindset, who believe that their ability level is set, tend to think that if something is difficult then it is because they simply aren't smart enough. They then avoid challenges because they don't want to risk finding something difficult with the blow that brings

to their self-esteem. This leads to a common picture of under-achievement of able people who give up readily rather than test themselves. Having a growth mindset, on the other hand, leads to people enjoying challenges and valuing opportunities to stretch themselves.

Dweck's advice for supporting a mastery orientation and growth mindset in children is to focus on the goal of learning, rather than on the level of outcome of their performance. She points out that each of our words and actions sends a message which tells children how to think about themselves. It can be a fixed mindset message saying 'You have permanent traits and I'm judging them,' or it can be a growth mindset message which says: "You are a developing person and I am interested in how you are developing'. We can avoid telling children they are clever or good at painting as if that is a fixed attribute, and instead focus on the process of what they are thinking and expressing. We can avoid praising children for achievements which are easy for them, and instead encourage children to take up challenges, praise them for their efforts, and help them to think about what they can learn when things go wrong. By showing children that we value their learning processes, we help them to reach confidently for the opportunities to learn.

The adult role in children's playing and exploring

The central question of what adults have to do with children's play and exploration deserves pause for reflection at this point. Clearly adults can be too present and controlling, diminishing the potential benefits of play in building the child's autonomy and explanatory drive. While the Foundation Stage framework for Wales calls for 'structured educational play', it also notes the risk that 'If play is structured/restricted in such a way that children are given no opportunity to select materials, friends or to develop their own ideas, they will stop playing.'[66]

The idea that play should be 'structured with clear aims for children's learning' shows little understanding of the child as the agent and director of their own learning. A teacher may plan a role play area on the theme of pirates, for instance, with the intention that children will develop their verbal narrative ability by acting out a story they have read together. But the children may take part with very different learning intentions: One is exploring how to become part of a social group, another is enthralled with the movement possibilities of sword play, another wants to see how it feels to dress up and become someone who is frightening and threatening, another wants to recreate scenes or ideas from Peter Pan or Pirates of the Caribbean. The concept of 'purposeful play' must recognise that children bring their own purposes – and that these are powerful because they are in the zone of each child's current learning agenda and at the edge of their capabilities.

Yet adults are a key resource for children's learning through play. In Scotland guidance for pre-birth to three describes the adult role in providing a play environment and interested adult presence: 'One of the most important aspects of supporting play is ensuring that children have the time, space and freedom to initiate, plan, lead and conclude their own play. Children tend to be most relaxed when they can play in the knowledge that members of staff are available and interested, as this enables children to invite staff involvement, or feel free to instigate interactions with staff.'[67] It may be, though, that adults going beyond availability to taking a more proactive role will be of more benefit.

  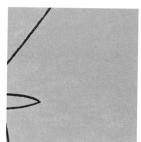

We have considered how the adult plays a useful part in stimulating and supporting exploratory play through introducing stimulating resources, sometimes briefly demonstrating possibilities, and inviting and supporting the child's autonomous and open-ended explorations. In imaginative play we have looked at the role of the adult in joining in to enrich the play and stimulate greater complexity when this is needed. Research indicates that teachers' participation in play can lead to greater complexity and to children remaining attentive for longer periods.

Children's view of themselves as competent and inquisitive learners is affected by whether or not they have an effect on things around them – whether there is contingency in their environment. It is an axiom for parents that 'Your child's best toy is you', and for early years practitioners that they are the most important resource in the early years setting. So it should not be surprising that an adult who responds to children's play and exploration in a contingent way is a more potent boost for autonomous learning than any responsive toy or material could be. We need to observe and support the child's purposes in their play, responding to their ideas and interests.

We need also to be observant about the quality and complexity of play, and where activity is routine and repetitious we can stimulate greater complexity by introducing problems to solve, by providing unexpected examples for children to ponder over and explore, and by using language that describes the process and highlights the learning ('You're trying to make the sand go through that hole, but it's stuck. I wonder what you will think to try next.') .

So how can words like 'planned' and 'structured' be usefully interpreted in relation to the open-ended nature of children's play'? In early years settings there is necessarily some structure surrounding play opportunities – it is not a laissez-faire situation of children turned outside to play on their own throughout the day. There is structure to the timing of play and other activities, and to the arrangement of available space and resources. There are also expectations about how space, time and resources will be used. Who will play is another element of structure – areas may have agreed limits on the number who can participate, children may be expected to share resources or may have control over whether they use them alone or with others, and adults may or may not be readily available for play. All of these elements are thoughtfully planned in effective settings, so while it is not possible to plan the content and specific outcomes of play it is good to **plan *for*** rich play and **structure** not play itself, but the opportunities for play.

Since play is not the only way in which children learn, it forms one part of a spectrum of learning activities in effective early years settings. Alongside adult support for and participation in play, effective practice also includes activities which are planned and structured by adults with specific learning outcomes in mind. While these are not play, they can usefully include some features of play in order to foster both children's subject learning and their development as learners. Justine Howard and colleagues have argued for adults to develop **playfulness**, an approach to interactions in all activities that blurs the boundaries between play and not-play and may harness the learning potential in children's natural propensity to play. Through considering what play looks like to a child they suggest that adults can capitalise on the high levels of motivation in play – through practices such as establishing a positive feeling of enjoyment, avoiding the habitual divide of presenting 'work' at tables and play elsewhere, adults becoming involved in all activities including play, emphasising processes and not products, and ensuring children perceive that they have choice and control in their activities.[68]

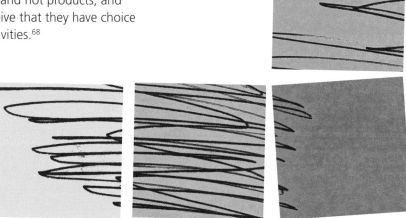

Playing and exploring – what might it look like?

Finding out and exploring
Playing with what they know
Being willing to 'have a go'

Consider how these children are playing and exploring.

Charlie, age 7 months

Charlie explores avidly with his hands, eyes, and mouth. He seems to be very interested in textures, touching and rubbing everything. He plays with his mother's hair when she holds him or has him in a backpack, and rubs and pushes food around on his highchair tray. In the garden he rubs the grass, and concentrates on the feeling of fluffy material.

He anticipates some play sequences, holding himself rigidly with excitement when his older brother plays a peek-a-boo game of 'Where's the baby?' with him, and erupts in laughter at the punch line. He also anticipates the excitement of a ball-rolling game he plays with his parents.

Charlie is keen to try new things, including reaching for and mouthing solid foods which he's recently been introduced to. He twists and turns to try to grab some paper he has seen a visitor holding. He is very eager to explore his brother's out-of-bounds Lego, and tries hard to reach it.

Chloe, age 2 ½

In water play with a range of containers, some with holes in the bottom, Chloe explored pouring water from one container to another. She observed closely, and then selected one with holes. She poured water into the container and held it up as she watched the water come through, and pointed out the holes to an interested adult.

Chloe participates in most activities in the setting, but seldom initiates and instead observes others before taking part. For example, she stood at one side without interacting to watch a peer chalking on a paper mounted on an easel. When the other child moved away Chloe picked up the chalk, looked at it closely and then began to make marks on the paper.

Jack, age 5

Jack had planned to play cars outside. He and his friends Luke and Callum were running around the perimeter fence. When the teacher came outside, Jack pointed to two fence sections: 'That's Llandudno and this is Ellesmere. I'm the Red Express.'

Teacher: I don't know what the Red Express is.

Jack: It means it's a big long train that goes very fast, and it's a red one.

Luke: And I'm a train. I'm Number 100.

Jack: I'm Number 50. You can go to Llandudno.

Teacher: Okay, I'll go. (She begins to move toward 'Llandudno'.)

Jack: Not yet. You catch a train to go to Llandudno. You haven't caught a train.

Callum: I'm the Number 4 train. (He walks slowly, pumping his arms like a steam train)

Teacher: The Number 4 train is a very steady train.

Jack: (racing past) I'm the express so I go very fast – just try to take a picture of me! When I went to Llandudno on holiday I went on a train. I'm coming now – quick! Get to the station and get on!

Callum: The Number 4 is going to Shrewsbury.

Teacher: When will it go?

Callum: In one hour.

Luke: The Number 4 is a slow train.

Teacher: I think I would like to go on a slow train.

Callum: Look, the Number 4 train is going there now.

Luke: You need a ticket.

Teacher: Where can I get a ticket?

Luke: In there. I'll be a ticket man. Here's your ticket. It costs £30.

Jack: You can jump on the fast train, but first get a ticket. The Red Express is going in his engine shed.

Teacher: I'll get a ticket for Shrewsbury, but how will I know when I'm at the right station?

Jack: We need some signs. (He uses some 'tickets' to write the town names, and tapes them to the fence.)

At review time, Jack described the play: 'We were the expresses, and the expresses can go fast and slow. And in the end there were carriages waiting. And when we need a rest we dropped the carriages off at the station, and another train can come and pick them up. Then we go in the engine shed to get some more carriages.'

How adults can support children's development as learners

Key messages for fostering playing and exploring

Provide an environment with:

- stimulating resources which are accessible, open-ended and can be used and combined in a variety of ways and are relevant to children's interests

- flexible space indoors and outdoors to explore, build, move

- limits to noise

- order and visual calm to aid concentration

- resources which the child can move, change and affect

- challenges appropriate to the development of the children.

Ensure children have uninterrupted time to play and explore.

Model and encourage open-ended exploratory play.

Watch, consider the child's intentions, and decide whether and when to support the child to manage what they are trying to do.

Give children opportunities to be independent in play, becoming involved only for specific reasons – to support, stimulate or extend when beneficial and for as long as needed to fulfil the purpose.

Join in play sensitively, fitting in with the children's existing play themes.

Act as 'play tutor' for children with little experience of imaginative play, modelling the next stage of developing dramatic play.

Model self-talk, describing your actions in play.

Encourage children to try new activities and to assess risks for themselves, giving positive messages with words and body language.

Focus on processes and not outcomes – not the end quality of what was produced, but the challenges faced, the effort, thought and learning involved, and the enjoyment.

Encourage a growth mindset, presenting failures as opportunities to learn and talking about how we get better at things through effort and practice.

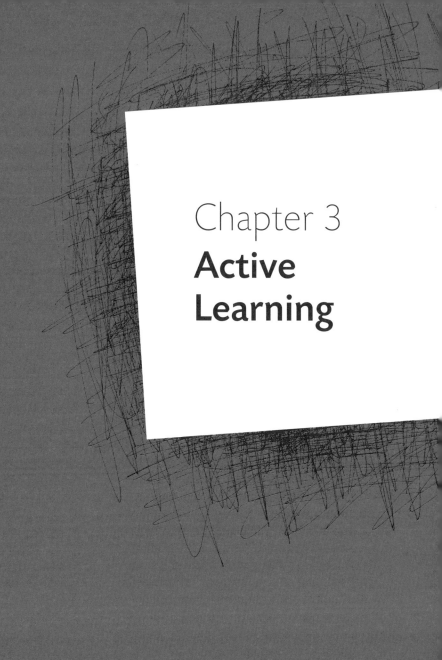

Chapter 3
Active Learning

Motivation

Learning is not something that is done to someone, but is achieved through active involvement of the learner. And the most effective learning involves not simple participation emotionally, mentally and – in the case of young children at least – physically. Learning is strongest when the learner also commits real energy, focuses towards a goal and demonstrates the tenacity to reach it. This active, energetic participation is the learner exhibiting the **will** to learn. In other words, the active learner is exercising a strong motivation for learning.

Effective learning does not always come easily. Even within the most interesting activities that excite our curiosity and provide enjoyment, there are likely to be points where we have to stick with a difficulty and keep trying to overcome obstacles in order to reach satisfaction. In fact, the most satisfying and motivating activities always involve a degree of challenge – otherwise they become routine and boring. There are also tasks, responsibilities, and lessons to be learned in life that do not in themselves excite our interest, but which we may believe are necessary and useful for another purpose. Will we have the motivation and self-control to persevere with difficulties and maintain our focus on our goals?

Motivation, like play, is a word which has been defined in many ways by theorists, perhaps not surprisingly because the ideas are intertwined with others presented in this book as the **engagement** of playing and exploring, and the **cognitive skills** in creating and thinking critically. So some theorists have defined it to include all those aspects of self-regulated learning, while others have looked more narrowly. For our purposes, I will consider motivation as the driving force that propels and maintains interest and engagement toward achieving a goal.

As Martha Bronson explains the importance of motivation, 'It gets physical, social, and cognitive activities started and keeps them going by providing both the direction or goal for action and the force necessary to sustain effort. Motivation is at the centre of self-regulation and must be considered in relation to the development of all forms of voluntary control.'[69]

That driving force toward particular goals has a resounding impact throughout our lives. The strength of our will enables us to apply and maintain effort to succeed in our studies and in our work. It also supports us to resist short-term attractions which conflict with our goal. For a small child this might mean ignoring the distractions of friends running past in a lively game when we are intent on gluing a model together, or resisting the urge to eat one marshmallow in return for the promise of two later on (see p70). As we grow up, the attractions of socialising with peers and indulging in risky behaviours may compete with our goal of doing well in school and work. The strength of our motivation, along with strategies to manage our behaviour, supports us to succeed.

Encouraging motivation for learning in children is critical not only to make the most of learning opportunities in the early years, but also because researchers find that motivation in childhood predicts motivation and success later in life, and is to some extent generalised across areas of endeavour.[70] One view is that motivation is a skill that children develop and carry with them over time and across contexts such as home, school, and peer relationships.[71] It is thought that young children begin with relatively high motivation which applies across all areas of learning, but motivation frequently declines as children go through school as well as becoming more specific to particular content areas. While some aspects of motivation are specific to the context, including both the learning environment and the content of activities, there are still basic attitudes which are linked to higher levels of motivation. Examining how attitudes promoting strong motivation for learning can be either supported or undermined will enable early years practitioners to ensure that they protect and foster children's natural motivation to learn.

Sources of motivation have received much attention by theorists and researchers, and some have already been discussed in terms of innate internal drives for competence, autonomy or control, relatedness, and making sense. There are also sources of motivation that come from outside of the person, which are described in behaviourist theory as reinforcers and punishments. These differing sources of motivation are related to motivation being described as either **intrinsic** or **extrinsic**. Intrinsic motivation arises from within the individual who is interested in the task for its own sake, while extrinsic motivation comes from outside with tasks performed as a means to an end, such as in order to gain rewards or avoid punishments. Evidence that intrinsic motivation is a better basis for effective learning provides important messages for early years educators. It is also necessary to consider the type of goals that children are motivated to achieve, since goals that focus on learning bring better outcomes.

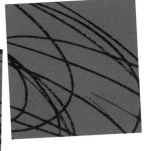

Being involved and concentrating

Logan, age 2, is playing with damp sand in a builder's tray. He uses a spade to pull the sand against the edge of the tray, bangs it flat and then pulls it into a pile again. He watches as another child brings a container of water and pours it into the tray, shifting some of the sand in its wake. Logan laughs and splashes his spade in the water, then stirs. 'More water!' he says, and goes in search of a bucket to bring water from the water tray. He pours it onto his pile of sand, and stands to watch the wet sand settle. 'More water!' he says again, and goes to bring more. He maintains his intense interest in this activity, moving and stirring pools of water and piles of sand even after the practitioner asks for no more water in the overflowing tray, for 20 minutes.

'I have no special talents. I am only passionately curious.'

Albert Einstein[72]

What leads someone to commit focussed attention and energy to an activity? It begins with an arousal of interest, which in some cases is easily satisfied by casual attention. But in other cases it develops into deep involvement in an experience, and sometimes into an abiding interest in a particular area over time. It is this more focused involvement that leads to learning.

The study of curiosity has shed some light on how people are pulled to expend energy and time on trying to reach understanding. Researchers have described curiosity as being initially aroused by noticing something different from what is expected. This links to an innate explanatory drive, governed by an internal need for consistency with any new information fitting into the understanding we have already constructed – our cognitive map. Something that does not make sense in terms of our existing understanding causes a tension known as cognitive dissonance, and arouses us to try to resolve the inconsistency by seeking more information. This links to Piaget's theories of assimilation and accommodation as the modes of cognitive development. In assimilation, we may adjust our perception of the new information to make it fit into our existing mental structures. But if we find that it will not fit with our existing ideas, then we may have to accommodate it by altering our cognitive map. Naturally we don't easily change concepts that we have invested mental energy in building up, so we may have to investigate the new phenomenon very carefully to find out whether it can after all be fitted in with how we already see things, or if we will have to go back to the cognitive drawing board and redraft our cognitive map.

Some people, though, will be initially attracted by the novelty of something unexpected but expend only limited energy in investigating it, while others will become deeply involved and concentrate on exploring the new phenomenon and resolving their curiosity. Researchers have found that two psychological traits work together to instigate and sustain deep rather than passing curiosity. One is the degree of openness to novelty and the other is a concern for orderliness, two traits which are not often strong in the same people. If people are open to novelty but not highly concerned with orderliness – which seems to relate to mental orderliness or cognitive consistency – they will show passing interest but not make the effort to find out how to reconcile the new information into their thinking. Those who are very concerned with orderliness often tend to be closed to new stimuli since they don't want to risk upsetting their cognitive map. Both will respond by avoiding close investigation so they can make assumptions that will fit, at least for the time being, with current understanding.

But highly curious people with both openness to something new and a strong need for cognitive consistency pay careful attention to the new stimuli, seeking more information and considering it from all angles, and in the process developing a much deeper understanding of the new stimulus as well as building a more stable and detailed cognitive map as they redraw its boundaries.[73] 'I like to think of curiosity as belonging at the border between chaos and cosmos,' write David Beswick. 'Highly curious people will remain longer than others in situations of uncertainty, as well as being more likely to be in such situations in the first place.'[74]

Learning at a deep level, then, requires a willingness to encounter and explore the uncertainty of something new, with the goal of making sense of the experience. The image of a young child deeply absorbed in their activity will be familiar to those who have used the involvement signals developed by Ferre Laevers as indicators of intense mental activity that indicates learning and development is taking place. Laevers believes that involvement is a necessary condition for deep level learning, and identifies observable signals of involvement including the child's concentration, energy, creativity, facial expression and posture, persistence, precision, reaction time, language and satisfaction.[75] Laevers describes involvement as 'strong motivation, fascination and total implication; there is no distance between person and activity, no calculation of possible benefits… The crucial point is that the satisfaction that goes along with involvement stems from one source, the exploratory drive, the need to get a better grip on reality, the intrinsic interest in how things and people are, the urge to experience and figure things out.'[76]

This level of involvement is similar to the concept of 'flow' developed by Mihalyi Csikszentmihalyi in studying adults in states of optimal experience. In a state of flow the experience becomes its own reward as the person becomes lost in the process, experiencing deep concentration and enjoyment, clarity about their goals and progress in what they are doing, no fear of failure, a feeling of control, and interest in the activity for its own sake.[77] Flow has been associated with increased performance in work, in sports, and in school.

There is much resonance across these ideas which throw a strong light on effective learning. Flow states have been found to be experienced more in people who seek novelty and also show persistence, which echoes the theory of deep curiosity. Flow is more likely in people with an internal locus of control, who feel they can control events and so can concentrate on internal drives rather than be concerned with the external demands of others. People with a strong flow motivation associate learning with positive feelings of curiosity, interest, excitement, concentration, absorption, challenge, variety, or stimulation, and the need to seek and master difficulties. And researchers have found that in adults flow motivation remains stable over time,[78] which is encouraging if we are able to protect and foster such habits of mind in young learners.

All of these ways of describing involvement in deep level learning involve intrinsic motivation – arising from within the learner, and engaging the commitment of the learner for the rewards of the activity itself. Flow is connected with embracing challenge and enjoyment of the process, but is decreased when there is pressure to achieve and when there are external tangible rewards. Intrinsic and extrinsic motivation will be discussed in more detail in a later section, but it is important here to link these ideas to the role of the educator in providing the conditions for deep involvement.

David Beswick, writing about curiosity, gives some guidance here: 'When people are intrinsically motivated they tend to be more aware of a wide range of phenomena, while giving careful attention to complexities, inconsistencies, novel events and unexpected possibilities. *They need time and freedom to make choices, to gather and process information, and have an appreciation of well finished and integrated products, all of which may lead to a greater depth of learning and more creative output.*'[79]

Ferre Laevers echoes this call for choice as a key factor in supporting higher levels of involvement for young learners: 'the more children can choose their own activities, the higher will be their level of involvement.'[80] The mounting evidence across many studies linking autonomy and choice with effective learning affirms the importance of children initiating their activity in the early years. When children choose and lead their activities they are able not only to follow momentary curiosity in novel stimuli which spark their interest, but to follow deeper drives for learning at the edge of their understanding, establishing their own level of challenge – to work in their individual zone of proximal development as described by Vygotsky. Adult-planned activities with specific learning objectives can never accurately fascinate and challenge all the children in a group. This was once expressed to me very clearly by a perceptive 8-year-old who was explaining why he valued the learner-initiated afternoons that had been instigated throughout his primary school: 'When the teacher plans a lesson, it's like she's decided what it will be and there are boundaries around how much you can do. But when it's child-initiated you can jump the fence.'

Choice, time and space, freedom to follow ideas without anxiety about an end product or external expectations, encouragement to remain at the uncertain border between curiosity and understanding without jumping to quick answers – these are all necessary for a child to experience deep concentration, and can be supported in the learning environment. Adults can also support children's absorptions by noticing what is fascinating to a child and planning to introduce materials and activities that will further challenge the child to engage in order to elaborate their understanding. In Reggio Emilia, these spurs to further involvement are known as provocations. Reflection on the nature of children's fascinations and thinking is at the heart of insightful planning in response to children's interests.

There is a developmental element to attention, with neurological maturation enabling children to more purposefully control their attention, and eventually to pay attention to more than one thing at the same time and to purposefully maintain focus on something that is not of their own choice. With even young babies, however, periods of deep concentration can be observed.

There are individual temperamental differences in concentration and distractibility, and some children find it more difficult to focus their attention. Purposeful control of attention can be supported in early stages by adults sensitively drawing children's focus to objects and events in the environment. Researchers have found that babies who focus more successfully on exploratory play have mothers who frequently stimulate their attention in a non-obtrusive way, effectively teaching the child to focus their own attention.[81] Supporting children to focus and maintain their attention involves an interactive dance of observing and responding to the individual child – stimulating interest where it is waning and may be refocused through shared attention, and calming an over-stimulated child.

Adults can support children to be learners who value the process of learning through establishing the conditions where children can experience the innately satisfying flow state. They can also explicitly acknowledge and encourage children's levels of concentration as they review children's activities together, helping children to understand the importance of committing their energy and focus to activities.

 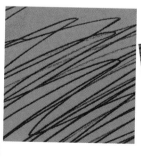 

Enjoying achieving what they set out to do

Anka, age 3, had left the small playground slide where her peers were playing, and stood watching the older children climbing up and whizzing down a much larger slide. Gail noticed her watching and said, 'Do you want to go on that one?' Anka nodded 'yes', so Gail said, 'Come on, I'll help you. You climb up and I will stay right here.' Anka climbed carefully to the top platform with Gail guarding her progress, but shook her head 'no' and stiffened when Gail invited her to slide down. She then sat at the top looking very pleased, as older children worked their way past her to slide down. 'Shall I help you down?' Gail asked, gesturing that she could lift Anka down, but Anka shook her head. After some minutes Gail again invited Anka to slide down, and Anka edged to the slope and slid down with Gail holding her hand. At the bottom she jumped onto her feet with a big smile on her face, and ran off to the smaller slide looking three inches taller.

'One should not pursue goals that are easily achieved. One must develop an instinct for what one can just barely achieve through one's greatest efforts.'

Albert Einstein[82]

If motivation is the force that propels us toward our goals, to understand motivation it is necessary to consider its complex relationship with goal-setting. When we are motivated to engage with an activity what sort of goal do we identify, why do we want to reach it, and does that matter to our learning and performance?

We have already touched on the ideas of intrinsic and extrinsic motivation, which relate to why we want to undertake activity. With intrinsic motivation the impetus comes from a desire to achieve satisfactions inherent in the activity itself – sheer enjoyment, and meeting personal internal drives. With extrinsic motivation the activity is undertaken not for its own sake but as a means to an end, because it will lead to something else not directly connected to the activity. There is plentiful evidence that intrinsic motivation is a better basis for learning and for achievements throughout life. Intrinsically motivated learners become more involved in their learning, using strategies more effectively and developing deeper understanding that they can apply in new situations. Intrinsic motivation has been linked to greater enjoyment, gaining greater knowledge and insight, and more persistence toward achieving goals.

It may be that babies and young children start out with an optimal degree of intrinsic motivation at birth. But it is a sad reflection on our schools that within a few years many children show less intrinsic motivation, and researchers say that the differences seen in older children are determined by what happens to them in their early years.[83] Bandura's theory of self-efficacy, the belief about whether or not we are capable of meeting our goals in particular situations, is interesting to consider in terms of very young children. Even though the concept of the self is still developing, very early in life we begin to identify and evaluate our own progress toward goals. Two-year-olds already know their capabilities, and show different reactions to their successes and failures according to whether they believe the task was challenging or easy for them – they show more pride with success in difficult tasks, and more shame in failing to manage easy tasks.[84]

There is certainly an emotional component to intrinsic motivation – we *enjoy* our achievements, and seeking a buzz from success spurs us on. Researchers Alison Gopnik and colleagues describe the emotional side of the explanatory drive: 'a deeply disturbing dissatisfaction when you can't make sense of things and a distinctive joy when you can. We can actually see those emotions on the faces of babies and young children. They purse their lips and wrinkle their brows when we present them with an object-permanence or false-belief problem, and then produce a radiant, even smug smile well before they actually give us the right answer.'[85] Practitioners from Pen Green nursery and children's centre in England observe toddlers for signs of 'chuffedness' – the body language which shows delight at having achieved something – sparked by work by Colwyn Trevarthen on tuning into the communications of babies and toddlers.[86] This is the sort of satisfaction I feel from completing a cryptic crossword – especially if I manage it by myself, though I'm nearly as chuffed when my husband and I do it together – even though it leads to nothing further since I expect never to send in a correct answer and win a prize. Perhaps the slight reinforcer of suggestions that cryptic crosswords might help to stave off Alzheimer's could be an external reward, but that is not what propels me to pick up the newspaper and seek out the puzzle that will tax me, require me to use a range of strategies, demand an investment of time and mental energy, and please me with the cleverness of the puzzle-setter, the fascination of watching my mental processes including overnight subconscious solutions, and eventual success in unravelling it.

Someone else puzzling over a crossword in their leisure time might, however, take a very different attitude to mine. They might rush to get hold of the first available copy of the newspaper and work feverishly to send off a completed answer every day, chalking up the number of times they were given a prize for the first correct solution received. They might even compare their success rate and speed with other crossword fans, maintaining a friendly competition.

So although two people may be engaged in exactly the same activity and achieve the same end result – a complete solution to a crossword puzzle, in this case – they may be motivated in very different ways and be working toward different goals.

What kind of goal?

According to goal theories, there are two basic types of goals which people pursue as they approach and engage in tasks – **mastery goals** (sometimes called learning goals), versus **performance goals**. Mastery goals include developing new skills, trying to understand, improving the level of competence, and achieving a sense of mastery based on self-referenced standards. Performance goals, on the other hand, involve judging the outcome based on how well one performs in comparison to others and receiving public recognition for performance. Mastery goals focus on engagement with the activity, while performance goals focus on the person's ability and self-image.

The link of mastery goals with intrinsic motivation is clear, with the marker for successful activity being whether or not participation in the activity meets internal competence and explanatory drives. Performance goals are more linked with extrinsic motivation, because success is not judged in terms of the activity for its own sake but is measured in external reward factors such as ratings, prizes, grades, or praise. This links, too, to Carol Dweck's work on mindsets – the growth mindset favouring mastery goals, while the fixed mindset is more concerned with showing a given ability level in comparison with others.

Not surprisingly, researchers find mastery goals consistently support people to learn and perform at a higher level than performance goals. Someone motivated to achieve mastery will have more real interest in learning the subject and will challenge themselves in relation to what they can achieve without worry about outside judgements, while someone concerned with the level of their performance may be more anxious about not looking incompetent in relation to others and become distracted from the point of the activity. Far from experiencing a state of flow and being totally engrossed in the activity, the performance-oriented person is always looking sideways to see how performance is measuring up. As learners go on in their studies, the mastery-oriented student will be interested to process new information, making links to other areas and curious about implications, while the performance-oriented learner is the one who decides whether to engage by asking, 'Is this going to be in the exam?' The performance-oriented learner may also limit their progress by avoiding challenge, opting out of things that might prove difficult to avoid the risk of looking incompetent if they don't measure up to others.

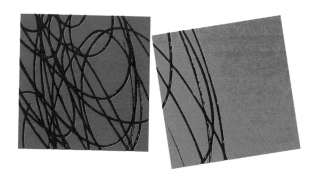

Whose goal is it? – the question of rewards and praise

People strive for mastery when they feel that what they do makes a difference, that they are competent to manage what they want to do, and that they have autonomy to choose the goal and how they are going to reach it. They are prey neither to learned helplessness nor to anxiety about their performance, but are interested in the process and believe they have control over it.

Richard DeCharms in his theory of personal causation described recognising oneself as an 'origin' of behaviour, rather than a 'pawn'. He showed that children can be taught to see themselves as origins of their own actions, bringing increased motivation, improved academic achievement evident years later, and higher rates of completing high school education. He worked with teachers and children on specific approaches geared around goal-setting and taking responsibility which sound remarkably like a High/Scope plan-do-review sequence: 'plan-choose-act-take responsibility'.[87] DeCharms stressed the importance of meaningful choices for students in determining their goals and the means to reach them, realistic assessment of abilities within the context of environment and others, and self-confidence about acting to reach the goal.

The importance of autonomy or control in goal-setting has been further developed in Self-Determination Theory. Deci and Ryan argue that motivation rests on an individual's innate needs for *autonomy*, *competence*, and *relatedness*. Our sense of self-determination is decreased if we perceive that the activity we are engaged in has been determined by someone else rather than being under our control, and our intrinsic motivation is diminished.

It is common practice in early years settings and schools to attempt to encourage positive behaviours by rewarding children, for example with stickers. Praise is another extrinsic reward, and frequent advice for parents and professionals is that we should be generous with praise. This is not as straightforward as often presented, however, because there is a risk that in using rewards and praise in an effort to build children's confidence and self-esteem we could instead inadvertently hinder their sense of self-determination and lower their intrinsic motivation. Attempting to promote positive behaviour in children through liberal use of external rewards is based on an assumption that children are not motivated unless the motivation is provided from outside. But if children are intrinsically motivated by a need for autonomy which includes setting their own goals, when adults convey a message through rewards and praise that the goal actually has been chosen by the adult then children identify less with the activity and become less motivated to participate.

An early example of studies in this area showed that when children expected and received a ribbon and gold star for drawing pictures, they later spent less time in the activity. Children who received no reward, or who received an award unexpectedly, in contrast continued to be intrinsically motivated to use the pens and draw pictures.[88] So one risk of giving external rewards is that the child turns away from the very behaviours we would like to encourage.

Bandura writes, 'goals can be applied in ways that breed dislikes rather than nurture interests. Personal standards promote interest when they create challenges and serve as guides for aspirations. But if goals assigned by others impose constraints and performance burdens, the pursuit can become aversive.'[89]

Another risk is that the child loses sight of mastery goals and intrinsic pleasure in the activity itself, and instead begins to focus on extrinsic motivation and move toward performance goals. If it feels good to be praised the child begins to 'perform' for adult approval, becoming what has been called a 'praise junkie'. I recall one four-year-old girl who would repeatedly dash off felt-tip drawings with little involvement, often reproducing stylized flowers and suns, and bring them to show me at regular intervals: 'Do you like my picture?' I would try to engage her in a discussion of colour or spatial choices she had made, or invite her to tell me about her picture, but she would immediately reply, 'But do you like it?' She would not be drawn, either, on any aspects *she* might like about her pictures and it was clear that the purpose they served for her was a chance to ask for praise unconnected with any real competence shown or her learning process.

The impact of extrinsic rewards, however, is not always negative and the context of using rewards and praise needs to be taken into account. In a large-scale analysis of 128 studies, Deci and colleagues found that extrinsic rewards significantly affected what children then chose to do, with stronger effects decreasing intrinsic motivation for younger children receiving

tangible rewards than for college students. But when external rewards were given only occasionally, and without being expected, they did not seem to reduce motivation, while rewards and praise that were linked not to simply taking part in the activity but instead gave clear feedback about the quality of the engagement were seen to improve intrinsic motivation.[90] If praise is used judiciously to draw attention to such things as how the learner is involved, concentrates, persists, uses different strategies, problem-solves and has independent ideas then it is actually reinforcing the role of the learner as the agent of their own learning. It gives useful feedback on competence, while acknowledging the autonomy of the learner in the quality of their performance of the task.

It is important that feedback is specific, and linked to behaviour. It is now generally understood that it is inappropriate and harmful to label a child as 'bad'. 'Label the behaviour, not the child' applies, so that while we would not say a child is 'naughty' we perhaps would say that we don't like a particular thing the child did, and explain why. Generally, however, the penny hasn't dropped to show the flip side: neither should we label a child as 'good', or give blanket approval to what the child does. Being told that you are 'good' or 'clever' at drawing, or building, or running or anything else helps to establish a fixed mindset rather than a growth mindset. You have been told that you have that ability, which is a burden to live up to and gives no support for ways of actually developing your competence. You can become hooked not on the challenge of growing more competent according to your own judgement, but instead on reassurances that you are 'good' and that your efforts are 'lovely' or 'well done' even if they did not really involve your best efforts at all.

Star charts to reinforce positive behaviour, usually reserved for managing challenging behaviour, are an example of extrinsic rewards which pose a risk of hindering a child's intrinsic motivation. Particularly when a larger tangible reward depends on obtaining a certain number of stars which are in the gift of the adult, a star chart removes the child's autonomy and focus on their responsibility for the true consequences of their behaviour. Behaving in a prescribed manner becomes linked to what it will earn. I have only once used a star chart as what felt like a last resort, with a nursery child whose challenging behaviour was persistently distressing to him, his family, peers and nursery staff. I was determined, however, that it be under his control and used as a marker of his self-control and progress. In a small book with each page divided into three sections to represent elements of the nursery morning, he was invited to choose from one to three stars to show how well he had taken part. His decisions were never questioned, but it gave a focus for his review and explanation, and for his key person to acknowledge how well he had concentrated, or played alongside or with others, and so on. Once or twice when he decided on only one star, explaining that he had kicked or hit someone, it still gave an opportunity for a learning conversation about the effects of his actions along with a fresh commitment to manage well in the next segment of the day. Within only a few days the novelty wore off and both he and his key person

started forgetting to use the book and stars – it faded away, but his improved self-control did not as he built more positive relationships and enjoyed the true rewards of being part of the nursery community.

Motivated through relationships

Being motivated by following one's own interests and setting personal goals could give the impression that learning is an individual, solitary affair. But this is far from the case. All development and learning take place in a context where the nature of social relationships is a key part. Deci and Ryan argue that self-determinism does not mean individualism, where everyone operates only on their own track toward their own goals. Instead, they say, the innate need for relatedness is a strong motivator. Relationships, particularly with important adults, provide the sense of well-being and emotional support that enable young children to risk attempting activities at the limits of their competence.

Peer relationships are also a significant factor in children's sense of self-efficacy. They learn about their own competence and are stimulated to become involved through observing and imitating other children. Warm social interactions can be a central part of why some activities are enjoyable. I have known children in an early years setting who, when they are asked to plan their activity, respond only that they are going to play with a particular friend – the type of play can be much less important than the fact that it would be together.

Belonging to a community supports motivation, and sometimes the sense of competence and the goal belongs not to one person but is shared across a group. In Reggio Emilia the group of children involved in a project share their intentions, their thinking and their ideas, in joint ownership of the learning. Adults document and reflect on the development of thinking across the group as a whole, rather than tracking individual children's development. As children become part of social groups, the need to relate to others has implications for managing individual impulses in the light of values and goals of the group.

Belonging to a community is also important in children moving from their own personal goals which could be seen as a limiting, selfish perspective to adopt and identify with the values and goals of their society. 'To a great extent the child learns what to want,' writes Martha Bronson.[91]

Moving beyond spontaneous interest

So far we have considered the importance of children being intrinsically motivated to follow their interests and choose challenges that capture their deepest curiosity and concentrated focus. There are, however, many areas of activity that are valuable but may not immediately seem interesting or enjoyable. And there is also a place for maintaining motivation in activities that may not be attractive in themselves but are a necessary step to longer-term goals. As adults who are guiding children's learning in skills that they will need as successful members of society, we have a responsibility to introduce and cultivate interest in things that children may not approach spontaneously.

Bandura writes, 'Most of the things people enjoy doing for their own sake originally held little or no interest for them. Children are not born innately interested in singing operatic arias, playing contrabassoons, solving mathematical equations, writing sonnets, or propelling shot-put balls through the air.' He discusses the process through which interests develop, mediated by feelings of personal effectiveness and satisfaction in reaching personal standards. 'There is nothing inherently gratifying about playing a tuba solo,' Bandura writes. 'To an aspiring tuba instrumentalist, however, a performance that fulfils a hoped-for standard is a source of considerable self-satisfaction that can sustain much tuba blowing.'[92] The hoped-for standard belongs to the individual, so there is personal satisfaction in achieving it, but personal standards are effective in building and sustaining motivation only if they are both realistic and challenging for the individual. Adults have a role in supporting children to break down complex skills into sub-goals where they can experience self-efficacy, leading to steadily growing personal involvement and interest.

Character is sometimes defined as what you do when no one is looking. This touches on the difference between intrinsic and extrinsic motivation, but it's not as simple as either-or. We also choose to go along with what others want us to do. Self-determinism theorists have considered the divide between intrinsic and extrinsic motivation, and argue that self-

regulated learning means both having high intrinsic motivation and also successfully managing extrinsically motivated behaviours – and that it is the responsibility of educators to support both of these. For example, studying for an exam may not be inherently interesting, but a student needs to be motivated by the longer-term goal of gaining a qualification that will enable them to do a job which they are intrinsically motivated to do. Bearing in mind an innate need for autonomy, theorists describe a continuum for extrinsic motivation. In this continuum, children gradually move from **complying** because of a promise of reward or threat of punishment, through feeling that they **ought** to comply in order to avoid feeling guilty or to win approval, and then to identifying that the activity has value for its usefulness in reaching their goals so they **choose** to act on it and feel they are in control. The final stage, which is unlikely to be reached by young children, is an integration of a social value into their own consistent web of values and goals, making it truly their own.[93]

I had a period of teaching in a women's prison, where the inmates perceived little or no autonomy. Prison rules allowed little choice, and in their lives as a whole the women often felt that they were the victims of circumstances rather than agents. The course was aimed at supporting the women, some as young as 16, to take control of their lives and build motivation to return to study. We used an interesting exercise in assertiveness, where they were asked to write three statements starting 'I have to...', three statements beginning 'I should...' and three beginning 'I need...' They found this very easy to do. All of these statements, however, reflect a passive outlook and extrinsic control over behaviour. I then asked them to change just one word in each

sentence: 'I have to' became 'I choose to', 'I should' became 'I could,' and 'I need' became 'I want'. They were startled at the change in the locus of control the new sentences showed. Particularly challenging were the discussions about 'I choose'. 'I *don't* choose to turn up on time for roll call – I have to,' they would say. But as we explored the sanctions and unravelled the consequences, they could acknowledge that they did have a choice.

The important thing to recognise was that choices come with responsibility to own your decisions about values and goals. Even in such a coercive environment, they could choose not to attend roll call, and to take the consequences such as loss of privileges or extra days on their sentence, if that was what they believed met their goal of independent autonomy. On the other hand, if their goal was a relatively easy time in prison and swift release, then compliance with prison rules could be their personal choice, acting autonomously within the circumstances. It was not a free choice, admittedly, but decisions always have consequences – and ownership of the goal and the means to reach it can be a powerful step toward personal control of behaviour in the face of extrinsic pressures.

This was an exceptionally coercive context in which to explore and support learners' sense of personal causation and self-determinism. It is interesting to recall the evidence that at-risk children who attended high quality early years settings at ages three and four were much less likely to find themselves in that situation as adults, which reinforces the significance of the early years in fostering children's sense of themselves as competent, in control and responsible for their own decisions and actions.

Keeping on trying

Lily, age 4, was excited to show practitioner Karen how she could skip rope. She needed two people to turn the rope so she asked a friend to hold one end and Karen the other. She tried repeatedly to jump at the right moment, but the friend wasn't able to hold the rope high enough for it to go over Lily's head. Lily wanted to keep trying, so Karen showed her how they could tie one end of the rope to the fence, making it high enough to go over Lily when Karen turned it. With careful turning and timing by Karen, Lily was able to jump the rope once or occasionally twice in succession and concentrated on this for a while with just a wry smile and sigh when she missed. Later Karen noticed that Lily had used the rope to tie a toy dog to the fence with a complicated series of knots, and was now trying to untie it. She worked at the knot diligently before coming to Karen to ask for help. Karen saw at a glance that there was only one final loop of the knot, so she said, 'You're nearly there. Can you see where you need to pull for that part to come through?' She then held the rope in place for Lily to complete the untangling. 'Yes! I got it!' Lily said with obvious satisfaction.

'The most important tool of the theoretical physicist is his wastebasket.'

Albert Einstein

Persistence is an essential trait for achieving success. The familiar phrase 'Try, try again', trumpets the value of keeping going, being resilient and maintaining motivation in the face of obstacles. Successful people are not those for whom everything comes easily, but are familiar with failure – as inventor Thomas Edison said, 'Many of life's failures are people who did not realise how close they were to success when they gave up.' J K Rowling, author of the phenomenally successful Harry Potter books, initially faced rejections from a dozen publishers before finding one prepared to take it on. But rather than consigning the manuscript to a drawer, she sent it to the fortunate thirteenth publisher.

Remaining undaunted by failures and maintaining motivation in the face of obstacles means staying engaged and ready to learn. Thomas Edison again, in reply to his discouraged assistant on yet another failure of a promising filament for electric light bulbs: 'I cheerily assured him that we had learned something. For we had a certainty that the thing couldn't be done that way, and that we would have to try some other way.'

There is a strong link between persistence and other habits of mind that form the characteristics of effective learning. People show more perseverance when they have a mastery orientation, a sense of autonomy and personal goals in their activities. They remain with activities longer and will try different ways of achieving their aim when they face difficulties, compared to others who quickly give up in the face of difficulties.

Babies and young children are familiar with the power of persistence – they practice their developing skills over and over until they succeed. A baby does not walk confidently on the day of taking first steps, and doesn't give up trying because of landing unceremoniously on their bottom time after time. Differences in persistence, however, appear very early. Some of the difference may be explained by a basis in inborn temperament, but also the ways in which adults interact with children has been shown to have an effect. Researchers who followed babies from age six months to 13 months found that the babies who were more persistent and focussed on goals at six months were more competent at 13 months. Aspects of their environment in their earliest months were significant: the babies who at six months experienced more stimulation and responsiveness from their mothers and had experiences of responsive toys were more likely to be persistent at 13 months.[95]

Another study compared parenting styles with babies' persistence and competence at 12 and 20 months, and concluded that the mothers' attitudes and behaviour affected babies' persistence at mastering their environment. Particularly important was mothers' behaviour in supporting their babies' autonomy in their activities, sensitively responding to their child's attempts rather than attempting to control them.[96] Support for autonomy included verbal information or feedback, and physical help such as holding a toy for the child to manipulate. Greater persistence was also linked to mothers offering sensitive care and having

more knowledge about child-rearing. More controlling mothers, on the other hand, tried to change what the baby was doing through such things as saying 'no', guiding the child's hand, or disapproving body language. The authors suggest that supporting a child's autonomy is particularly important at this stage when children need to develop the sense that they can make a difference in the world, and they cite other studies linking adult support for autonomy in one-, two- and four-year-olds with children feeling responsible and in control of their actions.

Believing that through continued effort you have the power to make a difference also ties in with having a growth versus fixed mindset. Carol Dweck has studied how primary-aged children responded to dealing with a difficult challenge in learning new material. She produced maths tasks with deliberately confusing material near the beginning of the activity paper. The children who were high-achievers in maths did very poorly on the rest of the task after having faced the section they couldn't manage, while children who were less high-achieving carried on successfully. The high-achievers couldn't cope with the confusion and panicked. In further studies Dweck showed that high-achievers often had a fixed mindset – believing that they were naturally gifted at maths, rather than needing to work for success – and became upset because they thought that being confused showed that they weren't gifted after all. This led them to give up trying, while children who had more experience of struggling had more motivational resources to keep trying.[97]

Children need opportunities to struggle, and to learn that persistence often pays off. Early years practitioners often focus on scaffolding children's learning, providing support and structuring tasks to ensure that children succeed. Guy Claxton cautions against missing opportunities to help children build learning power: 'Helping (children) learn better is not the same as helping them become better learners. Effective support can easily create dependency, unless the teacher is continually looking for opportunities to dismantle the scaffolding, and build student's disposition to do their own supporting.' Echoing the lessons from supporting babies to build learning power, he says that the intention should be 'always to look for a way to do less, to hand the control back to the students'.[98]

Manageable challenges, with encouragement to keep trying, are an important practice ground for developing persistence. One young boy in nursery was accustomed to ready assistance from his parents, who would greet his efforts with 'Are you struggling? Here, I'll do it.' One day he approached me with a long face and his twisted jacket hanging from one arm and said, 'I'm struggling with this.' He was surprised – as was his father when I recounted the incident at the end of the day – when I replied, 'That's good! If you really struggle you can probably sort it out.' Then I helped him by talking through how he could find the other armhole and put the coat on by himself. His father acknowledged that he had never looked at it that way, and that perhaps they could support their son's continuing efforts rather than jumping in to help too quickly.

Staying on track – delayed gratification

Being able to keep on trying *not* to do something is also an important ability that enables the learner to reach a goal, through resisting temptation to switch to an easier or more immediately attractive alternative. When researchers compared persistence in toddlers, they found that two-year-olds who lacked persistence often dealt with a challenge by changing the task to something easier. Sometimes the competing alternative to reaching a goal may promise immediate pleasure, and it's hard to avoid succumbing to the short-term temptation at the expense of longer-term and more important goals. But delaying gratification is an important life skill, enabling you to study even though your friends are going out, maintaining a work schedule even though you're ready for a drink, saving money for an important goal even when there are new fashions you haven't caught up with.

Experiments of young children's ability to delay gratification were conducted by Walter Mischel at Stanford University in 1972 – the marshmallow tests. Four-year-olds were shown a marshmallow on a plate in front of them, and told that if they sat in the chair without eating the marshmallow until the researcher came back in 15 or 20 minutes he would give them two marshmallows. If they didn't want to wait, they could eat the marshmallow and ring a bell at any time and the researcher would come back but there would not be another marshmallow. One third of the children ate the first marshmallow right away. Another third resisted temptation for a few minutes, but then gave in and ate the marshmallow. But some children were able to control the urge to eat the marshmallow in front of them, waiting successfully to double the treat later.[99] The researchers followed up the children in adolescence, and found that the children who were able to wait for two marshmallows were dependable and well-adjusted teenagers who could cope with problems and make good relationships, while those who couldn't wait were more likely to have behaviour and social problems. There was also much higher academic achievement among the children who had waited.

These experiments are often cited as explorations of will-power, but according to Mischel there is another critical ability at play. 'What we're really measuring with the marshmallows isn't will power or self-control,' Mischel says. 'It's much more important than that. This task forces kids to find a way to make the situation work for them… We can't control the world, but we can control how we think about it.'[100] The children who were able to resist the marshmallow were able to control their attention through a number of strategies – covering their eyes, singing songs, tapping rhythms on the table – to distract themselves from the power of the temptation. Mischel has since found that children can be taught mental strategies like this, such as pretending the marshmallow is only a picture, and children who hadn't been able to wait for even one minute could then wait for fifteen.

In other words, controlling thinking is what makes the difference. The children who could wait had discovered a strategy to control their thinking, and it is a key point that such strategies can be taught. This 'thinking about thinking', or metacognition, is a crucial part of self-regulated learning which will be at the core of the next chapter.

The adult role in children's active learning

Important adults are a major factor in the context in which children shape their view of themselves acting in the world. It can be helpful to consider the adult role in meeting each of the basic needs identified as autonomy, competence, and relatedness.

The central place of supporting children's autonomy in helping them to build strong motivation is clear. Adults provide effective support for a child's autonomy when they provide practical, verbal and emotional help for the child to work toward his or her own purposes. A growing sense of autonomy is fostered through valuing children's feelings and points of view, and ensuring that children have opportunities to make choices and decisions. Children can be encouraged to take responsibilities that are appropriate for their age in real meaningful tasks. Strong intrinsic motivation can be built by capitalising on children's fascinations, providing opportunities for them to make decisions about how to follow their interest in activities that engage them. Help is given to enable children to be successful, with an awareness of giving less support as soon as the child is able to engage in the task independently.

A sense of competence grows when children have opportunities to take part in challenging activities, in which they can engage for the intrinsic pleasure of the activity itself and judge their success against their own personal standards. Adults can support children's awareness of competence by encouraging children to set their own goals and reflect on their own success, and by giving meaningful and explicit feedback about the processes that support their successful achievements.

Relatedness, and its connection to emotional well-being, underlies development and learning. Specifically in terms of the development of motivation for learning, there is abundant evidence that the quality of interactions in warm, supportive relationships can help children to know that their ideas are important, and that they can be active and make things happen. Relationships with adults and peers also contribute to the intrinsic enjoyment of activities. Adults can plan opportunities which enable children to work and play together, and can help to build a sense of community learning together. Adults also support children's sense of relatedness when they help children to internalise social rules and help children to build self-control in their behaviour with others. Supporting children in a problem-solving approach to behaviour and conflicts helps provide tools for children be effective in relating independently to others. Adult talk has a crucial place – using language to provide reasons for expectations about behaviour, to talk through consequences, and to give prompts for managing behaviour helps children to gradually identify with the values and goals of their community and to participate successfully.

Active Learning – what might it look like?

Being involved and concentrating
Enjoying achieving what they set out to do
Keeping on trying

Consider how these children are demonstrating active learning.

Charlie, age 7 months

Charlie focuses and concentrates intently on toys that respond to his actions. He has a flower toy which sticks to his highchair tray, and he is able to make parts of it spin or revolve. He ignores people around him as he uses his hand and index finger to make the toy respond. His mother says he has a cot toy which has buttons which move in different ways, and he spends several minutes at a time focussing on how to make them move. Even when he doesn't manage at first, he keeps trying to copy the movements his father has shown him.

Charlie loves visits from his grandmother, and is eager for her attention when she arrives. He holds out his arms to her, and responds with big smiles when his action is effective and causes his grandmother to pick him up.

Chloe, age 2 ½

Chloe took herself to the bathroom, and said to the adult Sarah who was already there, 'Want a wee.' She took down her trousers and pants by herself and sat on the potty. She stood up knowing that she hadn't done a wee, but was full of smiles at having managed the process. Sarah acknowledged her success: 'You had a good try on the potty all by yourself.'

Chloe likes to help with routines in nursery, such as preparing the table for lunchtime and tidying up toys. She wanted to help get resources out of the outdoor shed, and pointed to the tractor. When she attempted to pull it out, the wheels became stuck in the doorway and on other toys. She shook and wiggled the tractor, and didn't give up when it was released only partway. When the wheels were finally released she pulled it out, and then continued to help with other resources.

Jack, age 5

Jack went to the book area and started turning pages of a large art book. He found a dramatic painting he was very interested in and decided to recreate it. He carried the book to the workshop area, and selected his materials. Jack worked on his painting for an entire session, mixing colours very purposefully and maintaining a keen interest. He looked carefully at the features of the painting in the book, and concentrated on the details in his own painting, talking about these as he worked: 'I'm doing the cracks. I have to put some blue on top and in the corner.'

The activity was totally Jack's idea, and he was very clear about what he wanted to do. Jack sets high standards for himself, and sometimes shows disappointment in what he achieves. He enjoys challenge, and in this task he showed determination and perseverance, trying hard to mix colours that he was satisfied with. At one point he lost the page in the art book and began to get frustrated. The teacher supported him to find it again by turning the pages: 'Tell me when you see it and I'll stop.'

When Jack finished his picture he stood back to admire it, and asked an adult to take a photograph. He found and placed a 'whizzy work' card alongside it, and at review time was proud to share his work.

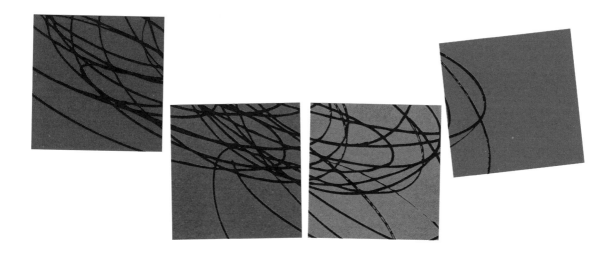

How adults can support children's development as learners
Key messages for fostering active learning

Observe and reflect on what arouses children's curiosity, looking for signs of deep involvement to identify learning that is intrinsically motivated.

Provide stimulating and novel resources and experiences related to children's interests to encourage involvement.

Enable children to exercise choice over their activities – setting their own goals and methods.

Ensure children have time and freedom to become deeply involved in activities.

Be aware of how children gradually gather and process of information, and help children to maintain their focus over time. Perhaps use photographs and talk about their activities, and keep significant activities in evidence rather than being routinely tidied away.

Support children to focus their attention, providing stimulation through shared attention or calming over-stimulated children as needed.

Help children to become aware of their own goals and to evaluate their own successes, by verbalising with the youngest children what you see them trying to do and then encouraging them to talk about their own processes and successes.

Avoid rewards that give control to the adult, and be cautious in using praise.

Recognising children's successes and showing an interest in how they approach what they are doing is a constructive reward.

Be explicit in giving feedback on behaviour that shows children's learning processes -- such as concentrating, trying different approaches, persisting, solving problems, and having new ideas.

Support and encourage relationships between peers, children teaching each other, and as a community learning together.

Help children to begin to identify with values of the community so that they are able to feel they choose to act in line with these. Give reasons and talk about consequences of behaviour, rather than giving commands.

Break down complex skills into subgoals, where children can enjoy success and build motivation for things that are not immediately attractive.

Encourage children to persist with difficulties, trying again or in a different way.

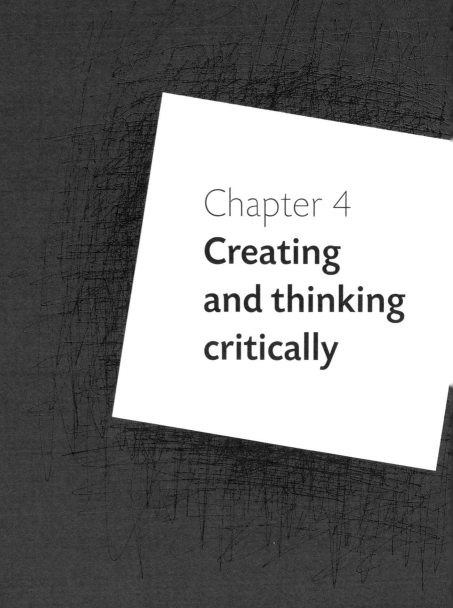

Chapter 4
**Creating
and thinking
critically**

Being strongly motivated sets children in motion and sustains them toward learning, but effective learning requires another essential ingredient – children need to be not only *willing* but also **able** to use and control their minds to process all the information and ideas they encounter. Effective learners move beyond unconscious mental processes to become aware of themselves as thinkers and learners, and they **learn how to think** about things in the most constructive ways.

People with the ability to think creatively and critically are being increasingly recognised as essential for a society to flourish. It's not enough to be able to memorise information and reproduce what we have been shown. Progress in areas that affect us all – in business, science, politics, the arts – depends on people who can find their way through information overload, think about interconnections, decide what is important, come up with new solutions to problems, identify the best ways to go about things, and explain and justify their reasoning. These skills are not specific to any one area of learning, but cut across all content areas. They include mental skills, such as abilities to consciously control attention, to plan, to use memory effectively, to monitor progress, and to notice inconsistencies and correct errors in thinking. Along with mental skills, creativity and critical thinking also rely on dispositions such as open-mindedness, flexibility, and regard for being reasonable and fair to other points of view.

Creativity and critical thinking are not the same thing, but they work together for people to be problem-solvers and respond to situations in innovative ways. Creativity can be thought of as the ability to think flexibly – to see things from different points of view and recognise multiple possibilities – and to come up with original ideas. It doesn't describe just the rare creative genius who changes the world's view with big ideas, but includes the creativity of finding new ways to think about and do everyday things. The original ideas may be new to the individual, but may well not be unique in the wider world – this is especially true for young children who haven't been exposed to ideas which may be current outside their experience. Creativity is sometimes assumed to relate especially to the arts, but it's important to recognise that creativity is a way of thinking which applies across all experiences and areas of learning. Critical thinking, on the other hand, involves rational approaches such as analysing information, comparing and classifying, using reasoning to draw conclusions, making decisions, evaluating thinking and ideas. When engaging in thoughtful goal-directed activities, from deciding how best to express an idea in a painting to how to deal with climate change, both creativity and critical thinking are needed.

Critical thinking is sometimes defined as including the skills of managing thinking and consciously deciding how to approach and sustain progress in a task. These are at the heart of self-regulated learning, which largely determines how well children achieve in school.[101] The skills are grouped and labelled in different ways by theorists, using such terms as cognitive control, executive control and metacognition ('thinking about thinking'). Thinking begins as an automatic process long before we have any awareness of it, and much of our thinking remains automatic throughout our lives as we process all the information arriving through our senses and call up memories to recognise people, things, situations, and so on. But being aware of, reflecting on and controlling our thinking is another layer that develops over time and leads to strongest learning capacity.

In terms of the developing brain, executive control or metacognition is believed to be governed by the frontal lobes, which form neural connections more slowly than other areas of the brain. The wiring of connections within the frontal lobes and to other parts of the brain becomes most dense during the second year of life, and the pruning process which selects the most-used, strongest connections to survive while others fade away occurs relatively late and only very gradually, continuing into adolescence. This is the last part of the brain to reach maturity, and it is our most recent evolutionary addition. Spending so long on developing the cognitive structures that enable us to think and learn most effectively gives people maximum opportunity to use all their experiences to build the brain structures needed to become able learners.

Based on Piaget's theory of developmental stages which saw young children as incapable of abstract thought, as well as evidence that young children find it difficult to identify what they remember or understand and to plan, in the past it has been considered that children did not develop metacognition until into the primary years. More recently, however, there is evidence that children from age three or four are beginning to talk about what they know

and think, plan and monitor their progress toward goals, and manage their attention and feelings as they solve problems. Even younger toddlers show emerging abilities to self-regulate their progress toward a goal, moving from using only trial-and-error in their activities to using strategies that they can apply in different situations, such as sorting or fitting things in other things.

Language – a prime tool for thinking

As adults, most of the time we keep our thoughts to ourselves while we maintain a running silent internal monologue of thought. When performing a complicated or unfamiliar series of actions, however, we have probably all experienced a boost to successful performance by 'thinking aloud' – repeating instructions out loud to ourselves in the right order, for example, to help us concentrate as we follow them one by one. For young children most activities which require control or sequences of behaviour make cognitive demands and their efforts, too, receive a boost by talking aloud to themselves. Theorists have identified this self-talk or 'private speech' which emerges in very young children as a key support in children beginning to control their actions and their thought.

The links of language to thought have been considered by many theorists, including Vygotsky who believed that language was central among the tools for higher level thinking that are passed down culturally to young learners.

Knowing a word for something helps us to think about it in a more general and abstract way, rather than being tied to the particular physical object immediately in front of us. For example, if we think that 'dog' is the individual name only for our family pet, but then learn that the same word applies to other furry four-legged animals it helps us to think about what they have in common which makes them fit into the same category. But since the neighbour's cat is not also called 'dog', we can puzzle over the similarities and differences and refine our ideas about both cats and dogs. In this way words themselves help us to develop concepts. This is true not only for understanding categories of objects, but also for more abstract ideas – if we talk with children about feeling sad, angry, worried, happy, excited, surprised, the vocabulary for feelings helps children to understand and identify their own feelings more accurately, as well as to identify them in others.

Vygotsky believed that children's private speech is the mechanism through which language helps children to develop their thought and self-regulation. As they label what they are doing in their private speech it helps them to see patterns and organise their behaviour, and then to plan and direct themselves. There is growing evidence that by the time private speech eventually goes underground in middle childhood to become internal mental comments on their own processes, it has played an important role in supporting children to be self-regulated thinkers. Possibly because it allows time and perspective for children to be aware of and control their behaviour rather than just react unconsciously, researchers have found links between private speech and delaying gratification, guiding one's own behaviour, problem-solving, coping with complex rules, regulating motivation and managing feelings.[102]

Just as talking to children about feelings helps them to recognise and manage their feelings more effectively, using the language of thinking and learning helps children to become more conscious thinkers. Important words and phrases – such as *think, know, remember, forget, idea, makes sense, plan, learn, find out, confused, figure out, trying to do* – can be part of the way we model for children our own processes of thinking and provide labels for what we observe in theirs, becoming significant keys for children to recognise and begin to control their own processes as thinkers.

Having their own ideas

'I know! I have a good idea!' says Gemma, age 5. 'This can be the carpet, and that one can be the sofa. Because he needs someplace to sit down. But if he wants to go to bed, we have to make him a bedroom. I think we need something else – maybe a box – for that because there aren't enough bricks.' 'No, not another room. He can sleep on the sofa because this is just going to be a little house,' says her friend. 'Okay,' Gemma says. 'But then it has to be longer so he can lay down.'

'Imagination is more important than knowledge. For knowledge is limited, whereas imagination embraces the entire world, stimulating progress, giving birth to evolution.'

Albert Einstein[103]

Thinking creatively in the early years opens a wellspring of enjoyment, and is integrally tied to play – playing with ideas, objects and people in an open-ended experience where possibilities abound. Anna Craft describes the heart of young children's creativity as 'possibility thinking', as children move from the straightforward question embedded in sensory play – 'what is this?' – to a more exploratory engagement with 'what if?', 'what could this be?', 'what can I or we do with this?'[104]

There are a number of qualities that come together in creative thinking. Imagination is needed to picture the possibility of something that doesn't already exist in the world. The creative thinker must also understand that there is more than one possible way to see the world, and more than one possible future. This divergent thinking requires openness to uncertainty and ambiguity, and being willing to suspend judgement while more possibilities are imagined and considered. The creative thinker also needs to respond well to the strong emotional aspects of creativity, which can bring pleasure and excitement in generating new ideas, as well as anxiety about taking a chance in suggesting or doing something new. And the creative thinker needs to be proactive in seeking the satisfaction of being an agent who can make things happen, shaping their world rather than simply accepting what is.

Creative process

Creativity has been the focus of much discussion in recent years, with debate and exploration of how education can best help children prepare for a lifetime of contributing to a developing and improving society and a vibrant and creative economy. A key report, *All Our Futures: Creativity, Culture and Education*, stressed that creativity has a place in all areas of human activity, and that everyone has the capacity to be creative. It placed an emphasis on the creative **process** including four elements: using imagination; pursuing purposes; being original; judging value.[105] Understanding the creative process will help early years practitioners to avoid focussing narrowly on a creative product. Young children's creativity often does not result in a final product, but it is important to recognise and promote children's facility in the stages in the creative process.

Imagination in the creative process is more than just creating a mental picture of something. It means using flexible thought to combine ideas in new ways, going beyond what is expected or routine to think of a new approach, and expanding from the known to something beyond. A fluent imagination will be able to generate multiple possibilities, which for young children often grow out of playing around and combining resources and actions in new ways.

Pursuing a purpose means that creativity doesn't happen in a vacuum – it is always in a context of doing or producing something. Creative ideas are in the service of something else, such as solving a problem, or expressing an idea, or creating a product. This doesn't mean, however, that creative activity is single-minded in pursuit of a goal. Anyone engaged in the creative process may discover new purposes and change their focus along the way, and this happens very readily for young children. As with scientific invention, a creative discovery may be made in trying to meet one purpose which turns out to be valuable for another purpose entirely, and certainly young children may rename a creation and refocus their activity more than once on route. While a final point may not be reached, creativity still occurs purposefully on the way toward something which is in the child's mind at the time of doing.

Young children's **originality** may not be the sort to have ground-breaking impact in the world at large. It means ideas which can be recognised as new to the individual child, and sometimes as being original in relation to their peers.

When original ideas have been generated, the final element of the creative process is **judging** whether they are useful in terms of the purpose. The creator evaluates whether they are relevant, compares various possible ideas, and decides on how to proceed. This is the point at which critical thinking intersects with creativity to complete the creative process, as the creator needs to step back and apply a different, reflective and analytical kind of thinking. Without this aspect many colourful but unfocussed ideas may be produced, but result in nothing of value. Within the creative process, the creator may need to move back and forth repeatedly between generating imaginative and original ideas, and evaluating and deciding which to pursue.

Within the creative process there may be moments of inspiration when good new ideas flow, and there is often a period of incubation when the possibilities and the purpose need to float around in the mind without active focus, to be returned to at a later time. During this time of mulling things over, new connections can be made bringing new creative insight. Practitioners who are aware that development of creative approaches may take time and can emerge in unexpected combinations can support children's interests over time, reminding them of previous approaches and encouraging them to make connections.

Creativity involves discovering and developing questions, not just answering them, which Anna Craft describes as an important part of 'possibility thinking'. Vivian Gussin Paley, a master of tracing children's thinking through their play and stories, writes that the difference between an adult dramatist and children creating a 'play' is that children are not concerned with a final product: 'They are always in Act One, on the first rungs of the ladder, preferring to linger there awhile. The children want to discover what the next question might be, before receiving too many answers from the grownups.'[106]

Structure and freedom

The interplay between children's freedom to initiate and control their own activities and the adult role in structuring learning opportunities is a key area of skilful practice. There is much evidence that shared control, blending adult guidance with a child's autonomy as the learner, leads to the best outcomes for children. It is the same picture in terms of developing creativity, where supporting children's creativity to flourish requires a careful balance between structure and freedom. Too much structure can stifle children's originality and their intrinsic motivation to think and create for themselves. Sadly, a common sight in early years settings is a display of identical pieces of 'artwork', copied from a model or assembled from a template prepared by the adult. These activities may provide practice in following instructions, or in fine motor skills, but usually appear in the adults' planning under a 'creative development' label when in fact they may instead undermine children's creativity. When considering planning an activity it is always worth asking the questions: Whose thinking is represented here? How much scope is there for children to find their own ways to represent and develop their own ideas?

Children will be asked to engage in adult-planned activities in all areas of learning and – since creativity can be developed within all areas of activity – when planned and presented well these can be opportunities for children to exercise the creative process. Incorporating an initial opportunity to play helps children to become more confident about approaching the task with divergent thinking, and leads to them later being more inventive and persistent at the task. One example of research in this area demonstrates that these benefits of play continue once children are in school. Children between the ages of five and seven were read a story, and then were asked to write a different story with one or more of the same characters. In preparation for the task some of the children were directly taught by the teacher, who showed

them story props and modelled story ideas. Other children played freely with the story props for ten minutes, while a control group were shown character cards but given no other guidance. The children then wrote their stories and later in the day recorded a story orally. The children who had played with the story props showed more originality and confidence than either of the other groups, while the children who had been taught appeared to show more anxiety and fear of failure which limited their creativity.[107]

On the other hand, providing *some* structure can support children to begin to organise their own ideas, and stimulate them to apply themselves to creative problems. Children can benefit from being shown techniques and possibilities, as long as they are shared as models of adults being involved in the creative process themselves – generating ideas which may or may not be selected and represent some possibilities among many. The art of skilled practitioners is in getting the right balance by providing a stimulus while supporting children's autonomy.

One study investigated the effects on children's creativity of setting limits in a painting activity. The children were given a paper lying on a larger paper and asked to paint 'a house you would like to live in'. They were encouraged to put anything in the picture they liked, and told it could be as 'make-believe' as they wanted it to be. The limits on the activity were then set in different ways. Some of the children were given no further guidelines. Others were given some guidelines which acknowledged other possible points of view while providing reasons for the expected approach: Although it is sometimes

fun to slop paint around, in this case the larger paper was to be kept clean so it could be used as a border, and also the brushes were to be washed before changing colours to keep them clean for other children to use. The last group of children were told 'the rules' about what they would 'have to do', and told to be a 'good boy/ girl' by keeping the paint off the large paper and washing the brushes. The researchers then compared the quality of the completed paintings in terms of creative ideas and competence, and the children's intrinsic motivation was measured in time they chose to spend painting afterwards and their reported enjoyment. They found that the rule-based controlling limits negatively affected children's creativity, quality of work, and intrinsic motivation. But when children were given information which helped them to internalise the guidelines, there was no difference between their creativity and motivation compared to the children who had been given no limits.[108]

Fostering creativity

Play is a key arena for developing the habits of mind needed for creativity. Through play the imagination is exercised, and many different ways forward can be offered, tried out and developed within the open-ended freedom to explore without risk of failure. Play belongs to the players, and so supports the sense of agency. Researcher Teresa Amabile has summed up her study of the conditions which allow creativity to flourish within the business world, which have many elements common with a good play environment: freedom for individuals to choose approaches to their work, failing occasionally without ridicule or punishment, stretching their horizons in working with others who share what they know, being supported with necessary resources. Without this context, she says, people will keep trying safe, repetitive approaches to solving problems.[109]

An enabling context for creativity, then, includes many of the same aspects already identified for supporting play and intrinsic motivation. Stimulating and flexible space and resources, time and opportunity to become immersed in experiences, choice and control, and relationships which offer opportunities to explore and spark together are all components of a provision that fosters creativity. The warm and supportive emotional environment, as in all aspects, is the bedrock of creativity, as a child needs to feel safe and confident to leave well-trodden paths and venture forward into new terrain.

Creativity is nurtured in an environment where questions are valued, different points of view are encouraged and resolutions are not sought too quickly. Adults can help children to articulate their own questions, as well as introducing stimulating and relevant creative problems to be solved. 'What else?' is an important question to support divergence and the fluent flow of ideas – What else could you try? What other ideas can we think of? Adults can reflect with children on their new ideas, and on why they are choosing or not choosing to do things in certain ways. Children can learn from important adults that just as in play, there is no 'right answer' in creative thought but that the process is valuable, enjoyable and interesting for its own sake.

Making links

> Grace, age 3, has been arranging pebbles and feathers on a light box in the nursery. She dips into a basket of resources, picks up a small, smooth pebble and says, 'Oh, it's cold.' She chooses another of a similar size and shape and says, 'And this one is cold.' She stops for a moment, thinks, and then points to the open door to the nursery garden. 'They've been outside. Or in the fridge.'

'One cannot help but be in awe when he contemplates the mysteries of eternity, of life, of the marvellous structure of reality. It is enough if one tries merely to comprehend a little of this mystery every day.'

Albert Einstein[110]

Within our complex world of objects, space, movement, people and all the relationships among these, human beings are active thinkers constantly making sense of their experiences. This begins in infants as a remarkably efficient automatic process, while learners for life maintain an outlook which continues consciously to make connections between different parts of our life experience and to search for meaning.

The brain of a newborn baby immediately begins to organise sensory information, searching for patterns, forming categories and making links between experiences. This mental processing quickly leads to recognising objects and people, making predictions, and associating cause and effect. Researchers are identifying key concepts that babies seem to be pre-programmed to develop, such as categories of living and non-living things, how objects behave in space, identifying individual sounds and patterns in spoken language, and understanding the nature of communication with others. Neuroscientists have proposed a theory of 'experience-expectant' learning, where brain structures are ready from birth to process certain types of input about the world and other people – quickly making sense of all the sensations of early life by building brain connections in response to experiences.[111]

Alongside the evidence of babies' abilities to make predictions described by psychologists, such as tiny babies showing puzzlement when objects travel out of sight behind a screen and reappear in the wrong place, observant caregivers will notice early examples of babies making links between events in their experience. A baby learns how to feed within only days of birth, when what began as a generalised rooting and sucking instinct has become a synchronised movement of turning, snuggling in and beginning to feed when held in position. Soon signals such as the mother adjusting her clothing will enable a baby to predict what is coming and join in the preparations for a feed.

In Martha Bronson's review of theories of developing self-regulation she refers to the instinct for self-control – the executive capacity supported by the brain's developing pre-frontal cortex. She explains that the intrinsic goals of the executive system appear to be three: to organise information so that it is meaningful, to be able to anticipate events, and to find a better or more interesting way to solve a problem or reach a goal.[112]

Although the brain may be ready and expecting experiences, the process of organising the information into concepts is a very dynamic one. It depends on constant to-and-fro between the mental expectations that have been built up and the next experience to compare it to. This relates to Piaget's theory of mental schema and the thinker's active role in comparing new experiences to see whether they fit in, or whether the existing mental map may need some adjustment. The original concept provides a starting point, but it is changed, developed and expanded through interaction with experience. Then the latest model of the mental map creates a new starting point for making sense of the next experience. So within the first few months of life babies have learned through linking and comparing their experiences to discriminate objects, people, colours, shapes, and sounds, to anticipate routines and act in particular ways in tune with familiar patterns.

Once babies begin to gain physical control, making sense of their experiences accelerates as they can actively explore and experiment rather than simply observe. Toddlers are driven to experiment again and again, repeating actions to test their understanding. They thrive in an environment which is orderly and has predictable routines. A chaotic environment makes it much more difficult to see patterns and make predictions, and may discourage the young thinker from trying to make sense of their world. They also need an optimum level of stimulation – a bare and uninteresting environment provides too little input for the growing mind to add to the picture so that concepts remain poorly formed, while too much input can overwhelm efforts to study and categorise it effectively. The child is looking for the next stepping stone from where they currently stand, and needs to find themselves neither in a dull backwater with no other boulders in sight, nor in a fast-flowing stream carrying many rafts which bounce past too quickly to be grasped.

Talking, thinking, sharing

Language adds another level to the ways children can think about and learn from their experiences. As well as using private speech as previously described to help clarify the patterns and categories in their minds, children's thinking is very powerfully developed through conversation. Through putting their experiences and thoughts into words, children have an opportunity to turn them around and consider how they might fit with other aspects of their understanding. Of course, adults have a key role to play as conversation partners. While some general principles can provide guidance, in every instance of the impromptu dance of conversation the effective adult is an active learner who is observing, listening and trying to understand the child's thinking, making a hypothesis of a helpful way forward, and experimenting to find a useful way to share the thinking. Every situation is different, and this role at the heart of teaching young children calls on the adult's willingness and abilities to have a go, take a risk, be creative, and make sense – in other words, to be a learner about the child's thinking and about learning and teaching.

Recently I was sitting on the middle log of three in a nursery garden, chatting with two three-year-old girls. Emily had a string, which she stretched horizontally across our laps and said, 'Let's measure our height. Oh, we're all the same long.' Keira, who was a taller child than Emily, pointed to us in turn saying, 'Middle, big, small.' I repeated her comment, pointing as I said, 'Yes, we are three sizes – middle, big, small.' Keira then looked at the string across our laps, and said 'But we're all the same.' 'Yes,' Emily concurred happily, 'we're the same.' Keira appeared dissatisfied with the 'measuring tape' contradicting the evidence of her eyes and common sense, and said, 'Sometimes you have to think all the way back to where you started, and then you'll know.' I was puzzled at this and asked, 'Did you say back to where you started? Where is that?' 'I used to be little,' Keira said. 'When it's June it's my birthday and then I will be four, and then I will be big.' Clearly Keira had not resolved the complicated relationships between the level of our laps when sitting on identical logs, actual body sizes, the strange abstraction of measuring tapes, change in size over time, and years in age. In verbalising these issues, however, she was able to identify the links to provide herself with greater food for continuing thought. As the adult I could have attempted to explain it all to her, but it would have removed from her the active role of making links and puzzling over relationships. And it would almost certainly have

been ineffective because it would have jumped over several stages of meaning-making – as if I had picked her up from her stepping stone and placed her far away down the stream, leaving her powerless to know where she was, how she got there or how she could use that pathway again. Instead when I stood up I simply said, 'Now we can see I'm much taller than you,' adding another piece for her to ponder in her continuing development as a thinker.

It is challenging to be effective as a conversational partner and co-thinker with young children, and we all have occasions where our approach misses the mark. We wonder whether we might have contributed in a more helpful way, or whether we were too dominating and cut off or diverted the child's thinking. Alongside possible lack of awareness of the importance of using talk to develop thinking, perhaps lack of confidence is one explanation for research findings that this is an area of practice which has been uncommon in early years settings.

Increased focus on developing thinking through talk has been prompted by the EPPE research in England (Effective Provision of Pre-School Education), which demonstrated that a key factor in high cognitive outcomes for children was the amount of 'sustained shared thinking' in early years settings. The researchers defined sustained shared thinking as 'any episode in which two or more individuals "work together" in an intellectual way to solve a problem, clarify a concept, evaluate activities, or extend a narrative'. Further exploration of practice even in the best settings, however, showed that there was little sustained shared thinking taking place, while only 5.5% of adults' questions were open questions which might lead to further thinking together. Most sustained shared thinking occurred in groups of two or three, with adults extending children's thinking in child-initiated activities.[113] In New Zealand, where early years practitioners are encouraged to support children's 'working theories', researchers looked at the extent to which educators interacted to support children's cognitive development. They found that practitioners were reluctant to interact, and even when they were aware of children's thinking they more often supported their theories through introducing resources than through listening and talking together.[114]

Without suggesting that there are easy answers to the sensitive decisions adults make in supporting children's thinking through talk, researchers in New Zealand have recently highlighted some useful issues and dilemmas to consider.[115] Working with practitioners to carefully evaluate and reflect on case studies, they discuss the question of whether every instance of children making sense counts as a working theory which should be actively engaged in by adults. Often children wonder about things in a passing way, in 'throwaway comments' or 'throwaway theories', while the child's real focus is on something else. It may be more appropriate to prioritise not the fleeting theories, but instead engage more purposefully in interests that children show developing over time. They also discuss approaches depending on whether a child's theory is 'working' or stable – if the child is satisfied for the time being with their level of understanding and not currently testing and exploring in relation to a particular

theory, should adults attempt to disrupt it and prompt further thought? Could this block a child from developing more complex theories, or even discourage theory-making if they are always shown to be wrong?

This raises the question of how comfortable adults are to leave children with inaccurate ideas about the world around them, rather than readily filling in gaps in a child's understanding by supplying facts. It is true that there are times when children want to know, and adults are a useful resource for children's knowledge either by showing, explaining, or helping children learn how to look for information in resources such as books or the internet. Not all information children turn over in their minds needs to be personally discovered, and by providing information in answer to a child's questions adults can contribute to the store of ideas the child is attempting to fit together. On the other hand, not all children's questions are necessarily seeking information. It may be that the child is 'thinking aloud' in clarifying their own question, rather than wanting an answer to be provided from outside. It can be unhelpful to provide a full explanation in order to correct a child's misconceptions. There may be value in allowing a time of uncertainty for children to gradually edit their theories and build not only a stronger and more complex understanding in the particular area of interest, but also have more practice in thinking for themselves.

The best guide may be to try to read the child's intentions. Is the child puzzling over ideas in a way that shows engagement of thought? Then the adult can support by trying to follow the child's thinking, being a sounding board for the child. This becomes an interaction of joint, authentic interest as the adult seeks along with the child to clarify ideas and questions. As in any genuine conversation, both are equal partners and contribute without taking control. Adult comments and questions can help to focus the child's thinking on their reasoning, including the links and contradictions. Young children don't always easily transfer their knowledge and skills from one situation to use in another, so adults can also support them to make the links by reminding them of what they did or said at other times or in other situations.

Useful questions and comments might include open-ended invitations to express ideas such as: 'What are you thinking about?' 'Why do you think that?' 'I remember what you said yesterday. You said…' 'What do you think would happen if..?' 'Did you notice what happened when you did that?' 'I wonder why he would do that.' 'I wonder what this could be for.' 'I've never seen one like this – have you?'

Adults can also add fuel to thought by contributing planned, linked experiences. It is important here, however, to try to read the child's intentions carefully rather than jumping to conclusions which highjack the direction of thought. For example, one winter's day toddlers outside were fascinated to watch the way their boots made footprints in the snow. They then helped to push the snow together as the practitioners constructed a snowman. The practitioners thought the children had been highly involved in the experiences in the snow and wanted to extend the learning, so planned

for the children to make 'snow pictures' the next day with cotton wool glued onto sheets of blue paper. I suspect that not one of the two-year-olds connected the gluing picture with the experience of snow. The adults had jumped in with their interpretation of how to represent snow – and even with an assumption that the children would want to represent it. They had left out the crucial step of trying to interpret what it was about the snow experience that had captured the children's fascination. Perhaps exploration of an ice block and crushed ice would have been more useful if the children had been most interested in the sensation of cold and changes of compacting or melting, or walking through flour sprinkled on the floor if leaving marks as you walk was fascinating and worthy of further exploration.

Since imitation is a great source of children's learning, adults who model their own thinking are a key support for children to copy learning behaviour and so experience being people who think for themselves. To be good models some adults may need to shift their own emphasis from **knowing** to **learning** – from already having learned in the past, to being a model of the process of making sense of experience. 'I don't know. I need to think about that.' 'I wonder what will happen if I try…' 'I'm curious about…' 'That's funny. I didn't think that would happen.' After all, we are all still learners and are still developing our own personal understanding of the world around us, ourselves and others. We can show children that we value and are enthusiastic about engaging in thinking and learning, for ourselves and as their partners.

Choosing ways to do things

Archie, age 4, has piled a large load of hollow wooden bricks into a wheelbarrow, and then added the contents of a sack of garden cobbles. He grasps the handles and tries to set off, but the wheelbarrow twists and spills sideways. Archie rights the barrow, and begins to repack it. His friend Deshi joins him in loading the barrow. When it is all packed Archie again starts off, but it leans dangerously to one side and he catches it just in time. 'Put the rocks in the middle,' Archie says, so they transfer the cobbles into the centre under the bricks. Archie sets off more successfully, but when it wobbles again as he hits a bump on the path he calls 'Deshi, come help! You hold the front.' They then progress successfully with Deshi walking backwards at the front of the barrow.

'Never memorize what you can look up in books. The value of a college education is not the learning of many facts but the training of the mind to think.'

Albert Einstein[116]

The most able learners are those who have learned to 'think about thinking', so that they are able to be in control of how they go about learning, solving problems, and approaching tasks. They have in their repertoire a number of strategies for approaching tasks or problems which they can apply in different situations. But they do not use these strategies automatically or just because they have been shown what to do. Instead they are aware of options and consciously choose the best way forward. They keep their goal in mind, think about how best to reach it and then monitor their progress, changing their strategy if things aren't going to plan. They are fully self-directing their learning.

'Thinking about thinking' is known as metacognition, and has been defined as 'the knowledge and control children have over their own thinking and learning activities'[117]. These two strands are both important – effective learners **know** about what they know and about how they learn and solve problems, and can **control** the way they think and learn by applying the skills and strategies they know. These form the core of being not only willing but also **able** to learn.

What self-regulated learners do in applying their metacognitive abilities is much the same as the role of the early years practitioners in supporting children's learning through a cycle of observation-assessment-planning. Observation entails close attention to children's behaviour within particular contexts, followed by assessment involving reflection and evaluation in terms of children's knowledge, skills, well-being, thinking, and so on. Planning is the response which is intended to support, challenge or extend the learning. Self-regulated learners are taking charge of this process to support their own learning. They notice what they are doing and deliberately behave in certain ways, assess how well they are progressing toward their goal, and evaluate whether to maintain the current approach or to plan another way forward.

Metacognitive ability develops gradually, and it may seem ambitious to look for awareness and control of their own learning in children in the early years. Yet although young children will not attain fully conscious control over their learning within their first few years, the roots of these abilities are developing and can be fostered in early years settings.

Babies even under a year old are beginning to show elements of cognitive control. In simple activities such as stacking toys, filling containers or using puzzles they can choose goals, use strategies to reach them, monitor progress, correct mistakes, and change strategies to another that they know or can think of.[118] Strategies are sequences of behaviour – the 'how' of doing things – which are developed to enable us to do things in more effective and efficient ways. A sequence of progressive stages has been suggested in how children approach a problem such as fitting pieces together or making a train track: the youngest children tend first to try physical force to make things fit, but then move to trying to correct an error by changing only the immediate element; finally they are able to re-consider the whole set and the relationships between them.[119]

Initially the main strategy used will be trial and error, and a young child is likely to try things in a fairly random way and to repeat the same efforts. As increasing maturity of the brain brings greater working memory capacity, alongside increasing experiences of what works, a child builds up knowledge of a set of strategies that can be purposefully selected according to the task. Strategies may be discovered through exploring and experimenting, or learned through imitating or interacting with others. The simple strategy of turning a puzzle piece to fit in a shape sorter, for example, can be demonstrated to a toddler with the language of 'turn it' helping to cement the strategy in the child's mind.

The way children choose from available strategies has been studied by Siegler who describes children's learning developing not in a linear fashion, but in overlapping waves. He found that children will adopt new strategies even when existing approaches are working well. But they don't simply move on by replacing older approaches with more powerful and sophisticated strategies. Instead the weaker strategies continue to be used alongside stronger ones, and children will select from them according to the difficulty of the task – often choosing older, tried-and-tested strategies when the task or problem is more difficult.[120]

By the age of about four, children are able to move beyond simple choice and make use of strategies, to consider more consciously their own thinking and to use simply theories to regulate their learning.[121] Children aged 3-5 have been shown to use metacognitive behaviour in problem-solving, including talking about what they know, and regulating their thinking, motivation and feelings[122], and pre-school children use metacognition to plan, monitor progress toward goals and persist at challenging tasks.[123] Children's growing ability to regulate their thinking parallels the development of Theory of Mind, a specific cognitive ability to understand that they and others have intentions, beliefs, knowledge and desires, and that the minds of others are not the same as their own. Theory of Mind is linked with empathy in the emotional realm, and with learning through imitation. Young babies have been shown to have some understanding of the intentions of others, but flexibly comprehending that different people have different knowledge and perspectives seems to consistently appear only around age four. Theory of Mind (always a 'theory' because we can never know first-hand about the mind of anyone else) would seem to support growing awareness of oneself as a thinker, with the understanding that there are many possible ways to think.

What kinds of strategies?

There are an infinite number of strategies, covering all the ways to do everything. Many are specific to particular activities, for example: when you do a jigsaw you can look for the same colour on different pieces and see if they fit together; when you tie a bow in your shoelace, use your finger to hold the base of the first loop while you wrap the lace around; to form most letters that have a vertical stroke, start at the top and bounce back up to do the next part; if you are counting a set of five objects it helps if you line them up and move them one at a time as you say each number, and when you are proficient at that you can just touch them one at a time. Strategies like these form part of the knowledge base that children draw on, and they are more successful if they can remember and call the strategies to mind when needed.

Other strategies are more general and describe ways to approach tasks in many areas. Problem-solving, for example, is a process that applies broadly across types of endeavour. Someone might be highly curious and motivated to be a problem-solver, but they also need strategies to approach and manage the process successfully. Strategies for problem-solving might include the sequence of: first identifying what the problem is; then gathering information about what is known and what is needed to be known to solve the problem; establishing a goal; making decisions about a plan of action, including steps along the way; putting the plans into action; checking how things are going; deciding whether it has been successful or whether more work is needed.

There are also strategies about learning and thinking, such as: remember that there is more than one way to think about things, so think of a few possibilities before you decide – playing about with it might help; think about whether you've done something similar to this before; if you practice something you will remember it better; repeating something out loud can help you remember it; keep checking to see whether all your information makes sense, whether there contradictions, and whether you understand it; other people can help you to think of good ideas; talking with others about what you are thinking helps you understand it better; sometimes you need to be determined and keep trying; if something doesn't work you can look for the reason and may need to think of a different way; you might concentrate better in a quieter place; taking a break and coming back later might help you start with a fresh focus.

Supporting children's self-regulated learning

Learning to learn involves knowing and using strategies effectively. Adults fairly readily share specific strategies for specific tasks, helping children to become more competent at particular skills and activities. But the underlying strategies about being a thinker and problem-solver may not be given as much attention, even though these are the powerful transferable skills that help children become successful lifelong learners. Can we directly teach strategies for thinking and problem-solving?

The short answer is that self-regulated learning can be directly supported through specific teaching. A review of 48 studies of programmes teaching strategies for self-regulation in primary schools demonstrated that these were effective, with children not only showing better achievement in content areas but also becoming more self-regulated.[124] But the authors point out that there were larger effects where the researchers delivered the programme rather than class teachers, suggesting that this is not an area where teachers are skilled, and that there is little well-researched guidance for teachers in promoting self-regulation. Three strands of effective programmes were identified: an integrated approach that included motivation as well as strategies; opportunities for children to practise strategies in meaningful contexts and receive feedback; and stimulation of reflection on the learning.

An integrated approach to supporting self-regulation in early years settings should naturally arise in an enabling environment, given the large overlap between the conditions that promote social and emotional well-being, playing and exploring, active learning, and creativity and critical thinking. Children's freely chosen activities are contexts for high motivation and divergent thinking, and are ready sources of real and meaningful problems and obstacles that children can identify and resolve. They are also sources of children's sense of autonomy and self-efficacy.

Explicit attention to highlighting learning strategies, feedback and reflection, however, is an area which may need development. Adults can support children to develop problem-solving strategies through, for instance, working through the process together on a group project, developing a mind-map to represent the steps in thinking about and carrying out plans. Helping children to talk about their ideas, plan, monitor and review can be part of daily structures. The plan-do-review sequence is a powerful tool which, when implemented well, can provide a strategy and regular practice and feedback on self-regulation for young children. Unfortunately the review aspect of this sequence is often neglected in busy early years settings, partly because of the challenges of managing it meaningfully. It may be appropriate and useful to verbally review in small key groups, so children can talk together and question and respond to each other, perhaps focusing on only one or two children at a time. Or the feedback and review can become an integral part of the adult's interaction with children at strategic points throughout their self-directed activities. As children review and become more aware of their own agency in conducting their learning, it supports a growing sense of self-efficacy as a learner.

Children learning together is another key resource in early years settings. A study among 3-5-year-olds found that metacognitive monitoring and control occurred most frequently during child-initiated activities, with children working in pairs or small groups with extensive collaboration and talk, but unsupervised by adults.[125] Children in cooperative play are working at the limits of their capabilities, and the need to share their thinking and coordinate activity is a spur to developing self-regulation. They also learn strategies from watching each other, and are more likely to imitate what someone quite like themselves does rather than an adult. Adults can support children to become involved together, and refer one child to another for help – and then decide when to leave them to develop their activity. Discussing afterwards what they did, thought, what worked and what didn't, will help to crystallise the strategies they used while maintaining children's ownership of the experience.

Talk, once again, makes a large contribution to supporting children's strategies. Children's self-talk helps them to guide their own activities. Bandura discusses the importance of children improvising their own self-guidance, which he says conveys a stronger sense of self-efficacy and agency than when simply repeating strategies taught by others. He recognises, though, that 'no amount of improvisational self-talk alone will create cognitive skills where they are grossly lacking.' The ideal for self-efficacy and thinking is to have been taught or learned strategies and then have opportunities to improvise how and when to use them.[126]

Talk also can bring the focus clearly onto the 'how' of learning. Guy Claxton writes:
'The teacher challenges students to think and talk about their own learning process with questions such as:

■ How did you do that?

■ How else could you have done that?

■ Who did that a different way?

■ What was hard about doing that?

■ What could you do when you are stuck on that?

■ How could you help someone else do that?

■ What would have made that easier for you?

■ How could I have taught that better?

■ How could you make that harder for yourself?'[127]

Questions such as these would be appropriate to students in colleges, and also for children in nurseries. They can become a regular feature of conversations with young children, as we turn our joint attention to what it means to be a learner.

Creating and thinking critically – what might it look like?

Having their own ideas
Making links
Choosing ways to do things

Consider how these children are creating and thinking critically.

Charlie, age 7 months

Charlie finds new solutions to problems he encounters. He is beginning to manage a pincer grip with food, but when he tried to eat a piece of cooked cabbage it was so floppy that he couldn't hold it upright to put into his mouth. When it got stuck wrapped onto his finger, he put his whole finger in his mouth so that he could suck the cabbage off it.

His mother has noticed him exploring opening his grasp to drop things. When they visited his grandparents he discovered that if he dropped bits of food from his highchair they would be eagerly eaten by the dog, and he was keen to continue this activity.

Charlie can move himself in a circle when he is on the floor on his tummy, but cannot yet move forward. He tries hard to reach his brother's toys, but when he shuffles on his stomach he only goes around in circles. When he has tried that for a while, he changes to a rolling motion and rolls to his goal, smiling and giggling when he reaches it.

Chloe, age 2 ½

Chloe was sitting on a large construction toy arch. She began to rock backwards and forwards, singing 'See-saw, see-saw'. Sarah asked her, 'Is it a swing?' Chloe shook her head. Sarah then asked, teasingly, 'Is it a… slide?' Chloe again shook her head. When Sarah asked, 'Is it a see-saw?', Chloe nodded her head and grinned.

Chloe then moved to ride on a tricycle, but kept coming across other vehicles and toys that were in her way. The first time she met an obstacle she first tried to steer round it, but was unable to turn successfully. She sat and looked at the obstacle briefly, then got off her bike and moved the obstruction before getting back on her bike and continuing on her way. She repeated the process on several occasions as she moved around the area.

Jack, age 5

Jack's idea to use a painting from an art book as a stimulus for him to paint was his own original thought. The painting in the book, a dramatic 'end of the world' scene, included mountains, a fiery red sky and dark billowing clouds, which Jack associated with his ideas about volcanoes and so he called it 'the lava picture'.

Previously in a focus activity the children had used large plastic roller trays to explore mixing colours, and Jack decided to make his picture by painting directly onto the tray rather than on paper. He was using a technique he had previously explored, but for a different purpose. He mixed colours carefully, and kept track of how well he was meeting his purpose by checking his work with the painting in the book until he was satisfied he had the right colours. He described the process he was using: 'I need more white to do the clouds.'

Jack's class regularly features a review of their activity by two or three children, and the children have learned to ask about the processes involved in the activity. At review time Jack responded to questions from his peers: 'Was anything tricky?' and 'What would you do next time?'

How adults can support children's development as learners
Key messages for fostering creating and thinking critically

Use the language of thinking and learning: *think, know, remember, forget, idea, makes sense, plan, learn, find out, confused, figure out, trying to do.*

Model being a thinker, showing that you don't always know, are curious and sometimes puzzled, and can think and find out.

Encourage divergent thinking: *What else* is possible?

Value questions, and many possible responses, without rushing toward answers too quickly.

Support children's interests over time, remind them of previous approaches and encourage them to make connections between their experiences.

Aim for a balance of structure and freedom, guiding but not controlling children's learning.

In planning activities, ask yourself: *Whose thinking is represented here? How will children find their own ways to represent and develop their own ideas?*

Build in opportunities for children to play with materials before using them in planned tasks.

Model the creative process, showing your thinking about some of the many possible ways forward.

Give reasons rather than directive 'rules' for any limits on children's activity.

Establish the enabling conditions for play: space, time, flexible resources, choice, control, supportive relationships.

Provide appropriate levels of stimulation within recognisable and predictable routines.

Be a sensitive conversational partner and co-thinker.

Plan linked experiences that follow what children are really thinking about.

Show and talk about strategies – how to do things – including problem-solving, thinking and learning. Use mind-maps to represent thinking together.

Give feedback and help children to review.

Encourage children to learn together and from each other.

Develop a learning community which focuses on **how** and not just what we are learning.

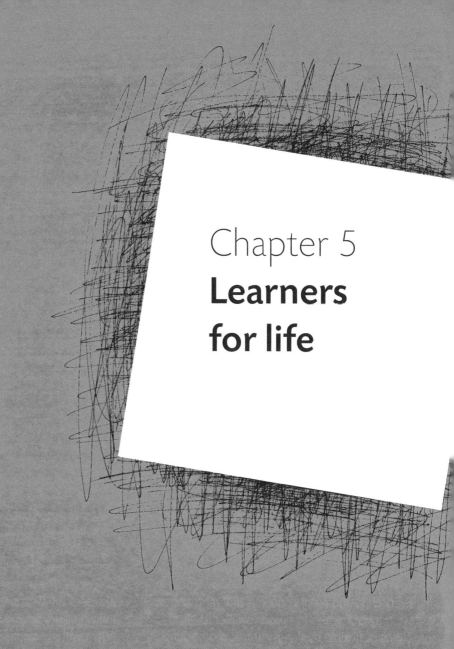

Chapter 5
Learners for life

"Not everything that counts can be counted, and not everything that can be counted counts."

Sign on Einstein's office wall, Princeton University

It is a straightforward matter to find out whether children can recite to ten, recognise their name, or label 2D shapes. Practitioners are familiar with assessing and recording children's attainment against a progression of knowledge and skills within all areas of learning. There is a risk, however, that the powerful cycle of observation-assessment-planning can become bogged down in focussing on easily identifiable pieces of information while missing things that really matter. If a curriculum-driven approach narrows to a subject-based emphasis on children's achievement, this sells short the opportunity to foster learning not just in content areas but, critically for children's long term future, in becoming more powerful learners.

Assessment of how well children are learning to learn may be unfamiliar, and puzzlingly less concrete than assessing skills and knowledge. Every child and every context is different, and we may lack scales to objectively plot levels of curiosity, flexible thinking, intrinsic motivation, creativity and self-directed learning. And, although the characteristics of effective learning will be seen in action differently at different ages and stages of development, in many ways they cannot be represented in a clear progression. A six-month-old baby can show the same degree of curiosity and intense interest as someone at six, sixteen or sixty. In fact, in some cases we would hope that older children and adults display at least as much motivation and focused learning as children in their early years and that their learning power has not been eroded over the years. We need to find ways to understand children's development as learners because what is noticed and assessed determines what we go on to support in our provision – and learning to learn should be perhaps our first priority as educators.

Learning to learn has been identified by the Education Council of the European Union as the most importance competence which people need throughout their lives for work, everyday activities and decision-making, and to participate as citizens in a knowledge economy and an inclusive and cohesive society.[128] The emphasis in education has moved away from simply handing down information, an approach which doesn't take account of the rapidly changing world where we cannot predict the type of knowledge that will be needed within a few years, let alone a lifetime. Competences for learning are emphasised because they go beyond skills and knowledge to look at how someone functions in real life situations, taking into account the whole person – feelings, attitudes, values, capacities and processes. The competence of learning to learn also sees the person in relation to others, with the individual developing an identity as an active learning agent within a community, where they can feel a common sense of purpose and feel recognised and valued in the group for their individual contribution and potential.[129]

Early years settings can be communities which support children to build stronger identities as learners, and can guard and foster their capacities to learn. How children are learning, not just what they learn, needs to move into the foreground of our attention. We need to understand why self-regulated learning is important, what it looks like, and how to establish our practice to support its development.

Decision-making in response to what we observe is the essence of professional skill in the early years. It applies to the times when we step back to think about our overall provision, and to plan activities. It also applies hundreds of times each day as we observe and interact with children on a moment-to-moment basis. We need to decide when and how we will engage with children, and a constant awareness of the child as learner will help us to make those decisions wisely.

We can observe what is happening in our settings, throughout the physical environment and throughout the day: Are children engaged in playing and exploring, are they motivated as active learners, are they thinking creatively and critically? Through reflection and discussion, practitioners can use this observation and assessment to determine improvements to provision and to our practice which might better support these processes. We can also reflect on learning characteristics shown by individual children. Would one child benefit from support to take a risk and try something new? Could another be particularly supported to plan, choose strategies, and review the success?

One practitioner who observed a young girl specifically to look for the characteristics of effective learning in action expressed surprise at what she learned: 'I thought I knew her, but perhaps she is not as confident as I thought she was. She was hesitant to initiate her own activities, almost as if she was not sure about permission to do things.' The setting makes observations recorded as Learning Stories, but while they refer to dispositions and attitudes the practitioner acknowledged that they are more aware of curricular achievements. 'We tend to notice the 'wow' moments, and I would have missed noticing how this quiet child deals with an obstacle if I hadn't been looking for it.' She then reflected on how she could support the child to 'bridge the gap' between her abilities and her confidence to have a go.

Guy Claxton describes the need for 'split-screen thinking', keeping part of your view on developing skills and knowledge within curriculum areas while the other part keeps an observant eye on learning to learn. Remaining aware of the potential of the messages we give to either support or undermine children's capacity to learn might help us to avoid clumsily rushing in to impose curricular 'next steps' at the expense of shoring up the foundations of a child's independent learning powers. It need not be a matter of one or the other. Children develop their learning powers while actively involved in activities – and these activities can be opportunities to gain more subject-specific skills and knowledge at the same time.

A further challenge and opportunity for early years settings is how best to share information and reflection on children as learners, and our role in that development, with parents who are our partners and the primary influence on children's learning and identities. This is a rich vein to explore together, highlighting and celebrating children's amazing capabilities from the beginnings of life and onward toward becoming lifelong learners.

A child learning: the characteristics of effective early childhood learning

Playing and exploring – engagement

Finding out and exploring

- Showing curiosity about objects, events and people
- Using senses to explore the world around them
- Engaging in open-ended activity
- Showing particular interests

Playing with what they know

- Pretending objects are things from their experience
- Representing their experiences in play
- Taking on a role in their play
- Acting out experiences with other people

Being willing to 'have a go'

- Initiating activities
- Seeking challenge
- Showing a 'can do' attitude
- Taking a risk, engaging in new experiences, and learning from failures

Active learning – motivation

Being involved and concentrating

- Maintaining focus on their activity for a period of time
- Showing high levels of energy, of fascination
- Not easily distracted
- Paying attention to details

Enjoying achieving what they set out to do

- Showing satisfaction in meeting their own goals
- Being proud of how they accomplished something – not just the end result

- Enjoying meeting challenges for their own sake rather than external rewards or praise

Keeping on trying

- Persisting with activity when difficulties occur
- Showing a belief that more effort or a different approach will pay off
- Trying hard

Creating and thinking critically – thinking

Having their own ideas

- Thinking of ideas
- Finding ways to solve problems
- Finding new ways to do things

Making links

- Making links and noticing patterns in their experience
- Making predictions
- Testing their ideas
- Developing ideas of grouping, sequences, cause and effect

Choosing ways to do things

- Planning, making decisions about how to approach a task and reach a goal
- Monitoring how effectively things are going
- Changing strategy as needed
- Reviewing how well the approach worked

Resources

Broadhead, Pat (2003)
Early Years Play and Learning,
Routledge

Broadhead, Pat, Howard, Justine,
Wood, Elizabeth (2010)
*Play and Learning in the Early Years: From
Research to Practice*,
Sage

Bronson, Martha (2000)
*Self-regulation in Early Childhood: Nature
and Nurture*,
Guilford Press, New York

Carr, Margaret (2001)
Assessment in Early Childhood Settings,
Sage, London.

*Finding and exploring young children's
fascinations: Strengthening the quality of gifted
and talented provision in the early years*, (2010)
Department for Children, Schools and Families,
Ref: 00107-2010BKT-EN

Gerhardt, Sue (2004)
*Why Love Matters: How affection shapes a
baby's brain*,
Routledge

Gopnik, Alison, Meltzoff,
Andrew, Kuhl, Patricia (1999)
How Babies Think,
Phoenix, London

*Learning, Playing and Interacting: Good practice
in the Early Years Foundation Stage*, (2009)
Department for Children, Schools and Families,
Qualifications and Curriculum Development
Agency Ref: 00775-2009BKT-EN

Moyles Janet, ed (2005),
The Excellence of Play, second edition,
Open University Press

Robson, Sue (2006)
*Developing Thinking and Understanding in
Young Children: An introduction for students*,
Routledge: Oxford

Tickell, Clare (2011)
*The Early Years: Foundations for life, health
and learning,: An Independent Report on the
Early Years Foundation Stage to Her Majesty's
Government*,
Department for Education

Whitebread, David (2011)
*Developmental Psychology & Early
Childhood Education*,
Sage

References

1 *Supporting Families in the Foundation Years*, Department for Education and Department of Health, 2011.

2 Bronson, M (2000) *Self-regulation in Early Childhood: Nature and Nurture*, Guilford Press, New York, 135.

3 Turney AH (1931) Intelligence, Motivation and Achievement, *Journal of Educational Psychology*, Vol 22(6), 426-434.

4 Duckworth, A, Matthews, M, Kelly, D (2007), Grit: Perseverance and Passion for Long-Term Goals, *Journal of Personality and Social Psychology*, Vol. 92, No. 6, 1087–1101.

5 Dignath, C., Buettner, G & Langfeldt, HP (2008) How can primary school students learn self-regulated learning strategies most effectively? A meta-analysis on self-regulation training programmes. *Educational Research Review*, 3, 101-130.

6 Geoffroy M-C et al (2010) Closing the gap in academic readiness and achievement: the role of early childcare. *Journal of Child Psychology and Psychiatry* 51(12): 1359–1367.

7 Sammons, P, Sylva K et al (2007) Effective Pre-school and Primary Education 3-11 Project (EPPE 3-11), Influences on Children's Attainment and Progress in Key Stage 2: Cognitive Outcomes in Year 5, *Research Brief No:* RB828 February 2007 ISBN 978 1 84478 890 3.

8 Reynolds AJ et al (2011). School-based early Childhood Education and Age-28 Well-Being: Effects by Timing, Dosage, and Subgroups. *Science* DOI: 10.1126.

9 Karnes, M B. Shwedel, A M, Williams, M B (1983). A comparison of five approaches for educating young children from low-income homes. In *Consortium for Longitudinal Studies* (Ed.), As the twig is bent : Lasting effects of preschool programs (pp. 133-169). Hillsdale, NJ: Lawrence Erlbaum Associates.

10 Schweinhart LJ (1997)The High/Scope Preschool Curriculum Comparison Study through Age 23., *Early Childhood Research Quarterly*, v12 n2,117-43.

11 Ibid.

12 Schweinhart LJ (2004)) *Lifetime effects: the High/Scope Perry Pre-School Project*, High/Scope.

13 Belfield CR et al (2006) The High/Scope Perry Preschool Program Cost–Benefit Analysis Using Data from the Age-40 Followup, *The Journal of Human Resources*, X L I.

14 Gerhardt, S (2004) *Why Love Matters: How affection shapes a baby's brain*, Routledge.

15 Tickell C (2011) *The Early Years: Foundations for life, health and learning,: An Independent Report on the Early Years Foundation Stage to Her Majesty's Government,* Department for Education, 86-91.

16 Carr M (2001) *Assessment in Early Childhood Settings*, Sage, London.

17 Claxton G (2002) *Building Learning Power*, TLO Limited, Bristol.

18 Whitebread D, Coltman P, Pasternak D, Sangster C, Grau V, Bingham S, Almeqdad Q, Demetriou D (2009) The development of two observational tools for assessing metacognition and self-regulated learning in young children, *Metacognition and Learning*, 4(1), 63-85.

19 Pascal C, Bertram T (2009) Accounting early for life-long learning. *Early Education*, no.57 (Spring) 10-11.

20 Bronson M (2000) *Self-regulation in Early Childhood: Nature and Nurture*, Guilford Press, New York.

21 Bronson M (2000), 41.

22 Bandura A (1994) Self-efficacy. In V.S. Ramachaudran (Ed), *Encyclopedia of human behavior* (Vol.4, pp. 71-81). New York: Academic Press. (Reprinted in H Friedman (Ed), *Encyclopedia of mental health*, San Diego: Academic Press, 1998).

23 UN General Assembly (1989), *Convention on the Rights of the Child*, Treaty Series, vol. 1577, 3.

24 Evangelou M, Sylva K, Kyriacou M, Wild M, Glenny G (2009) *Early Years Learning and Development Literature Review*, DCSF-RR176.

25 Adams S, Alexander E, Drummond M, Moyles J (2004) *Inside the Foundation Stage: Recreating the Reception Year*, ATL Research Report.

26 Wood L, Bennett N (1997) The Rhetoric and Reality of Play: Teachers' Thinking and Classroom Practice, *Early Years* Vol 17, Issue 2 1997, 22-27.

27 Loughton T, Teather S (2010) Creating conditions: trusted professional and targeted resources for creativity in the early years, *Born Creative*, Demos, 47.

28 Tickell C (2011) *The Early Years: Foundations for life, health and learning,: An Independent Report on the Early Years Foundation Stage to Her Majesty's Government*, Department for Education.

29 Welsh Assembly Government, Department for Children, Education, Lifelong Learning and Skills (2008) Play/Active Learning: Overview for 3 to7-year-olds, 7.

30 Northern Ireland Curriculum (2006) *Understanding the Foundation Stage*, Early Years Interboard Group, 6.

31 Howard J, Bellin W, Rees V (2002) Eliciting children's perceptions of play and exploiting playfulness to maximise learning in the early years classroom, Paper presented at the Annual Conference of the British Educational Research Association, Exeter, 12-14 September 2002 .

32 Murray L, Andrews A (2005) *The Social Baby: Understanding Babies' Communication from Birth*, CP Publishing, Richmond.

33 Gopnik A, Meltzoff A, Kuhl P (1999) *How Babies Think*, Phoenix, London, 33.

34 Evangelou et al, 52-53.

35 Bennett N, Wood E, Rogers S (1997) *Teaching Through Play*, Open University Press.

36 Moyles J (1989) *Just Playing: The role and status of play in early childhood education*, Open University Press.

37 Department for Children, Schools and Families, Qualifications and Curriculum Development Agency (2009) *Learning, Playing and Interacting: Good practice in the Early Years Foundation Stage*, Ref: 00775-2009BKT-EN.

38 Einstein A (1936) Physics and Reality, J*ournal of the Franklin Institute* Vol. 221, Issue 3.

39 Gopnik A, Meltzoff A, Kuhl P (1999) *How Babies Think*, Phoenix, 85.

40 Ibid. 71

41 Carlton M, Winsler A (1998) Fostering Intrinsic Motivation in Early Childhood Classrooms, *Early Childhood Education Journal*, Vol 25, No 3, 1998.

42 Gopnick et al (1999), 74.

43 Lewis M, Alessandri SM, Sullivan MW (1990). Violation of expectancy, loss of control, and anger expressions in young infants. *Developmental Psychology*, 26, 745-751.

44 Caruso D (2004) Dimensions of quality in infants' exploratory behavior: Relationships to problem-solving ability, *Infant Behaviour and Development* 16:4, 441-454.

45 Sylva K, Bruner J, Genova P (1976) the role of play in the problem solving of children aged 3-5 years, in J Bruner, A Jolly and K Sylva (eds) Play: *Its Role in Development and Evolution*.

46 Van Aken M, Riksen-Walraven JM (1992) Parental Support and the Development of Competence in Children, *International Journal of Behavioral Development* 15:1, 101-123.

47 Carlton M, Winsler A (1998) Fostering Intrinsic Motivation in Early Childhood Classrooms, *Early Childhood Education Journal*, 25:3, 159-166.

48 Bonawitz E, Shafto P, Gweon H, Goodman ND, Spelke E, Schulz L (2011) The double-edged sword of pedagogy: Instruction limits spontaneous exploration and discovery, *Cognition* 120:3, 322-330.

49 Buchsbaum D, Gopnik A, Griffiths T, Shafto P (2011) Children's imitation of causal action sequences is influenced by statistical and pedagogical evidence, *Cognition*.

50 Sitemaker.umich.edu/365.omo/parental_involvement.

51 Cited as conversation between Einstein and János Plesch in János: *The Story of a Doctor* (1947), by János Plesch, translated by Edward FitzGerald

52 Paley VG (2004) *A Child's Work: the Importance of Fantasy Play*, University of Chicago Press, 17.

53 Da Graca M, Dias BB, Roazzi A, O'Brien D, Harris P (2005), Logical Reasoning and Fantasy Contexts: Eliminating Differences between Children with and without Experience in School, *Interamerican Journal of Psychology*, Vol. 39, Num. 1, 13-22.

54 Broadhead, P (2003) *Early Years Play and Learning*, Routledge.

55 Elias, C L, & Berk, L E (2002). Self-regulation in young children: Is there a role for sociodramatic play? *Early Childhood Research Quarterly*, 17, 1–17.

56 Berk, LE, Mann, TD, Ogan, AT (2005) Make-Believe Play: Wellspring for Development of Self-Regulation, http://powerlib.net/makebelieveplayandselfregulation-4339.htm

57 Holland, P (2003) *We don't play with guns here: War, weapon and superhero play in the early years*, Open University Press.

58 Einstein, A (1930) Letter to his son Eduard (5 February 1930), as quoted in Isaacson W, *Einstein: His Life and Universe*, 367.

59 Bandura, A (1994) Self-efficacy. In VS Ramachaudran (Ed.) E*ncyclopedia of human behaviour*, Vol 4, 71-81.

60 Bandura, A (2001) Social Cognitive Theory: An Agentic Perspective, *Annual Review Psychology* 2001.52, 1-26.

61 Sorce, JF, Emde, RN, Campos, J J, Klinnert, MD (1985) Maternal emotional signaling: Its effect on the visual cliff behavior of 1-year-olds, *Developmental Psychology*, Vol 21(1), Jan 1985, 195-200.

[62] Hornik, R, Risenhoover, N, Gunnar, M (1987) The Effects of Maternal Positive, Neutral, and Negative Affective Communications on Infant Responses to New Toys, *Child Development* Vol. 58, No. 4 (Aug., 1987), 937-944

[63] Watson, J, Ramey, C (1969) Reactions to response-contingent stimulation in early infancy. Revision of paper presented at biennial meeting of the Society for Research in Child Development, Santa Monica, California, March 1969.

[64] Grolnick, W, Frodi, A, Bridges, L (1984) Maternal Control Style and the Mastery Motivation of One-year-olds, *Infant Mental Health Journal*, Vol. 5 No 2, 72-82.

[65] Dweck, C (2006) Mindset: *the New Psychology of Success, Random House*: New York.

[66] Welsh Assembly Government (2008) Play/Active Learning: Overview for 3 to 7-year-olds, Department for Children, Education, and Lifelong Skills, Ref: AC/GM/0838 January ISBN: 978 0 7504 4547 4.

[67] Learning and Teaching Scotland (2010) *Pre-birth to Three: Positive Outcomes for Scotland's Children and Families National Guidance*, ISBN: 978-184399-184-7.

[68] Howard J, Bellin W, Rees V (2002) Eliciting children's perceptions of play and exploiting playfulness to maximise learning in the early years classroom, Paper presented at the Annual Conference of the British Educational Research Association, University of Exeter, England, 12-14 September 2002.

[69] Bronson M (2000), p. 5.

[70] Lai E (2011) Motivation: A Literature Review, Research Report, Pearson, 14.

[71] Grolnick WS, Kurowski C, Gurland S (1999) Family Processes and the Development of Children's Self-Regulation, *Educational Psychologist*, 34(1), 3-14.

[72] Einstein A, Letter to Carl Seelig (11 March 1952), Einstein Archives 39-013.

[73] Beswick D (2000) An Introduction to the Study of Curiosity, Centre for Applied Educational Research, University of Melbourne, presentation at St Hilda's College Senior Common Room, Fellows night, 10 May 2000.

[74] Beswick, D (2000) Management implications of the interaction between intrinsic motivation and extrinsic rewards, www.beswick.info/psychres/management.htm.

[75] Laevers F (1999) The project Experiential Education: Concepts and experiences at the level of context, process and outcome. Katholieke Universiteit Leuven/Centre for Experiential Education: Leuven.

[76] Laevers F (2000) 'Forward to basics! Deep-level learning and the experiential approach', *Early Years*, vol 20:2, 20–29.

[77] Csikszentmihalyi M (2000) *Beyond boredom and anxiety. Experiencing flow in work and play*. San Francisco: Jossey-Bass. (Original work published 1975).

[78] Baumann N., Scheffer D. (2010). Seeking flow in the achievement domain: The achievement flow motive behind flow experience. *Motivation and Emotion*, 34.

[79] Beswick D (2000) op. cit.

[80] Laevers F (2000), 26.

[81] Carlton M and Winsler A (1998), 162-163.

[82] Einstein A, quote to Walter Daellenbach, May 31, 1915.

[83] Carlton M, Winsler A (1998), p 160.

[84] Lewis M, Alessandri SM, Sullivan MW (1992) Differences in shame and pride as a function of children's gender and task difficulty. *Child development*, 63, 630-638.

[85] Gopnik A (1999),162.

[86] Trevarthen C (2005) First things first: infants make good use of the sympathetic rhythm of imitation, without reason or language, *Journal of Child Psychotherapy* Vol 31:1, 91-113.

[87] DeCharms, R (1977) Students need not be pawns, Theory Into Practice 16(4), 296-301.

[88] Lepper, MR, Greene, D, Nisbett, RE (1973) Undermining children's intrinsic interest with extrinsic rewards: A test of the overjustification hypothesis. *Journal of Personality and Social Psychology*, 28 (1), 129-137.

[89] Bandura, A (1994).

[90] Deci, EL, Koestner, R, Ryan, RM (1999). A meta-analytic review of experiments examining the effects of extrinsic rewards on intrinsic motivation. *Psychological Bulletin*, 125(6), 627-668.

[91] Bronson M (2000), 33.

[92] Bandura A (1994).

[93] Grolnick WS et al (1999)

[94] Brecher K (1979)Albert Einstein: 14 March, 1879—18 April, 1955: A guide for the perplexed, *Nature* 278, 215-218

[95] Yarrow L, Morgan G, Jennings K, Harmon R, Gaiter, J (1982) Infants' persistence at tasks: Relationships to cognitive functioning and early experience. *Infant Behaviour and Development* 5:2-4, 131-141.

[96] Grolnick W, et al (1994).

[97] Dweck C (2006) Is Math a Gift? Beliefs That Put Females at Risk, in S.J. Ceci & W. Williams (Eds.) (2006); *Why aren't more women in science? Top researchers debate the evidence*. Washington, DC: American Psychological Association.

[98] Claxton G (2006) Expanding the capacity to learn: A new end for education? Opening Keynote Address, British Educational Research Association Annual Conference, September 6 2006.

[99] Patterson, C., & Mischel, W. (1976). Effects of temptation-inhibiting and task-facilitating plans on self-control. *Journal of Personality and Social Psychology*, 33(2), 209-217.

[100] Lehrer, J (2009) DON'T!: The secret of self-control, *New Yorker* May 18 2009.

[101] Bronson (2000), 135-136.

[102] Bronson (2000), 152.

[103] Originally in *"What Life Means to Einstein,"* Saturday Evening Post, October 26, 1929; reprinted in "On Science," in *Cosmic Religion*, 97.

[104] Croft, A (2007) Creativity and Possibility in the Early Years, TACTYC Reflection, http://www.tactyc.org.uk/pdfs/Reflection-craft.pdf.

[105] National Advisory Committee on Creative and Cultural Education (1999) *All Our Futures: Creativity, Culture and Education*. London: Department for Education and Employment.

[106] Paley,VG (2004) 75.

[107] Whitebread D, Jameson H (2005) Play, storytelling and creative writing, in Moyles J, *The Excellence of Play*, second edition, Open University Press, 59-71.

[108] Koestner R, Ryan RM, Bernieri F, Holt K (1984) Setting limits on children's behavior: The differential effects of controlling vs. informational styles on intrinsic motivation and creativity, *Journal of Personality* 52:3, 233-248.

[109] Amabile T (1999). How to kill creativity. *Harvard Business Review*, 76:5, 77-87.

[110] From the memoirs of William Miller, quoted in *Life* magazine, May 2, 1955; 281.

[111] Hall, J. (2005) *Neuroscience and Education, A review of the contribution of brain science to teaching and learning* SCRE Research Report.

[112] Bronson M (2000) p 149.

[113] Siraj-Blachford I (2010) A focus on pedagogy: Case studies of effective practice. In *Early childhood matters. Evidence from the Effective Pre-school and Primary Education Project*, ed Sylva K et al, 149-156. London: Routledge.

[114] Meade A (2000) If you say it three times, is it true? Critical use of research in early childhood education. *International Journal of Early Years Education* 8, no.1, 15-26.

[115] Peters S, Davis K (2011) Fostering children's working theories: pedagogic issues and dilemmas in New Zealand, *Early Years* Vol. 31, No. 1, 5-17.

[116] Frank P (1947) Einstein: *His Life and Times* (1947),185

[117] Cross DR, Paris SG (1988). Developmental and instructional analysis of children's metacognition and reading comprehension. *Journal of Educational Psychology*, 80(2), 131.

[118] Bronson (2000), 130.

[119] Robson S (2006) *Developing Thinking and Understanding in Young Children: An introduction for students*, Oxford: Routledge.

[120] Siegler RS (2005). Children's learning. *American Psychologist*, 60, 769-778.

[121] Schraw G, Moshman D (1995). *Metocognitive theories*. *Educational Psychology Review*, 7(4), 351-371.

[122] Whitebread D, Coltman P, Pino Pasternak D, Sangster C, Grau V, Bingham S, Almeqdad Q, Demetrious D (2009). The development of two observational tools for assessing metacognition and self-regulated learning in young children. *Metacognition and Learning*, 4(1), 63-85.

[123] McLeod L (1997) Young children and metacognition: Do we know what they know? And if so, what do we do about it? *Australian Journal of Early Childhood*, 22(2), 6-11.

[124] Dignath C, Buettner G, Langfeldt HP. (2008) How can primary school students learn self-regulated learning strategies most effectively? A meta-analysis of self-regulation training programmes. *Educational Research Review*, 3, 101-130.

[125] Whitebread D, Bingham, S, Grau V, Pino Pasternak D, Sangster C (2007) Development of Metacognition and Self-Regulated Learning in Young Children: Role of Collaborative and Peer-Assisted Learning, *Journal of Cognitive Education and Psychology* Vol 6:3, 433-455.

[126] Bandura A. (1994).

[127] Claxton G. (2006), 8.

[128] Council (2006), Recommendation of the European Parliament and of the Council of 18 December 2006 on Key competences for lifelong learning, (2006/962) *Official Journal of the European Union*. EC. Brussels.

[129] Hoskins B, Crick R (2008) Learning to Learn and Civic Competences: different currencies or two sides of the same coin? *JRC Scientific and Technical Reports*, European Commission.

Index